MATERNAL BODY

MATERNAL BODY

A Theology of Incarnation from the Christian East

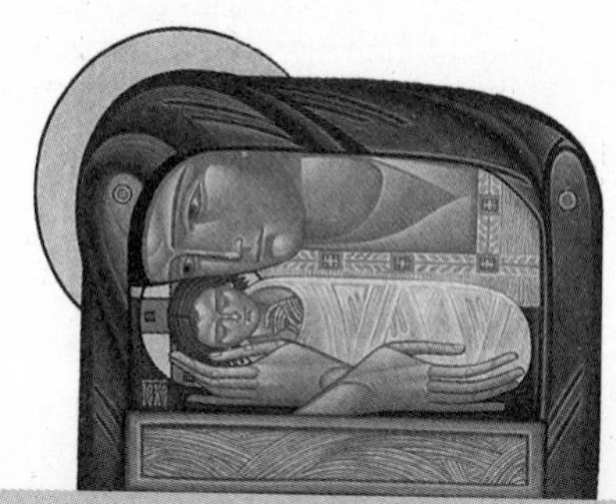

CARRIE FREDERICK FROST
FOREWORD BY JULIE HANLON RUBIO

Paulist Press
New York / Mahwah, NJ

Image credits: See page viii.

Cover image: *Nativity* by Lyuba Yatskiv, Contemporary Sacred Art Gallery IconArt, iconart.com.ua. Used by permission.
Cover design and book design by Sharyn Banks

Library of Congress Cataloging-in-Publication Data

Names: Frost, Carrie Frederick, author.
Title: Maternal body : a theology of Incarnation from the Christian East /Carrie Frederick Frost.
Description: New York : Paulist Press, 2019. | Includes bibliographical references and index.
Identifiers: LCCN 2018042718 (print) | LCCN 2018056735 (ebook) | ISBN 9781587687624 (ebook) | ISBN 9780809153916 (pbk. : alk. paper)
Subjects: LCSH: Women—Religious aspects—Orthodox Eastern Church. | Women in the Orthodox Eastern Church. | Orthodox Eastern Church—Doctrines.
Classification: LCC BX342.5 (ebook) | LCC BX342.5 .F767 2019 (print) | DDC 230/.19082—dc23
LC record available at https://lccn.loc.gov/2018042718

ISBN 978-0-8091-5391-6 (paperback)
ISBN 978-1-58768-762-4 (e-book)

Published by Paulist Press
997 Macarthur Boulevard
Mahwah, New Jersey 07430

www.paulistpress.com

Printed and bound in the
United States of America

For those for whom I am mother:
Cyrus, Ann, Eliza, Beatrix, and Ignatius;
for my mother, Menodora, of eternal memory;
and for all mothers everywhere

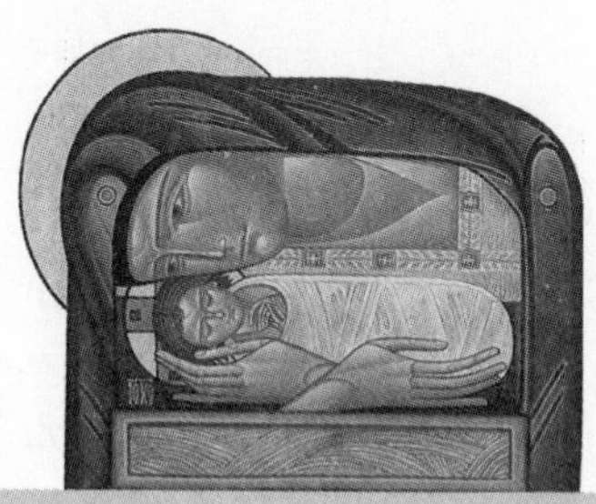

CONTENTS

Icon illustrations placed in center of book

LIST OF ILLUSTRATIONS

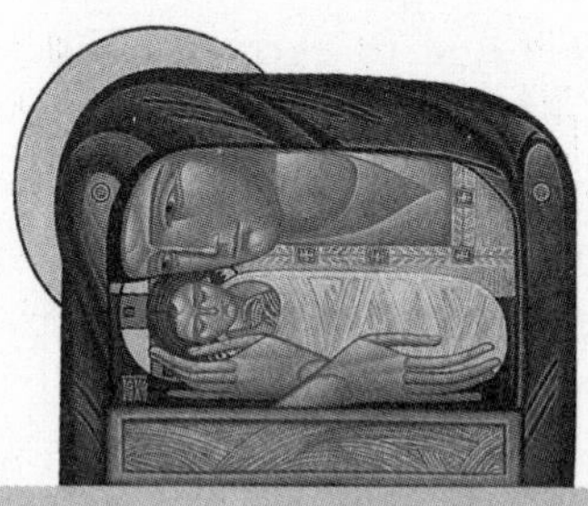

FOREWORD

I first met Carrie Frost in 2016 at a conference on marriage and family sponsored by the Huffington Ecumenical Institute at Loyola Marymount University in Los Angeles. The Institute asked three female theologians—one Protestant, one Orthodox, and one Catholic—to give the major talks. Our respondents were clergymen from our respective traditions. I asked for a picture of the three of us women seated together in the front of the auditorium. Though I have been writing about marriage and family for over twenty years, I had never been a part of an all-female panel, and this grouping seemed particularly important: three theologian mothers from the three major branches of Christianity addressing a room full of clergy and laypeople on the theology of marriage and family. I wondered, Had this ever happened before?

In her book on motherhood, Frost presents readers with something new, both because of who she is and because of how she thinks. As a mother of five, she brings life experiences that differ from those of the vast majority of theologians who have ever written. Finally, we have a woman who knows what it feels like to carry a child (or three!) in her womb, reflecting on central Christian stories involving conception, pregnancy, and birth. Frost's experiences as a mother lead her to turn her theological training to subjects that have rarely been considered in depth, to wonder about things few theologians have wondered about before: What knowledge of God might be gained from the pregnant maternal body? If Mary is Theotokos (or Birthgiver of God), what does that suggest about deification? What is the theological significance of nursing and weaning a child? How might Christians emulate Mary's "embodied contemplation"?

To answer these questions, Frost weaves together insights from the Christian tradition and her own experiences as a mother. As she mines the tradition, she often turns to prayers, hymns, and icons as well as to "theology" proper. Though the great thinkers of the Christian tradition, such as Saint John Chrysostom, offer some thoughts on motherhood, the material is not extensive. There is much more to be found in hymns and icons, where theology is taught in a more popular key. Frost's use of these sources raises the question "Where does theology come from?" As she expertly interprets images and lyrics, she shows readers that even if those entrusted with the official theological thinking missed opportunities to reflect on motherhood, Christian art, poetry, and songs often filled in the gaps. These sources, together with sermons, essays, and books, have contributed to theological reflection in the church, and readers who see this are invited to continue the conversation in light of their own experiences.

Throughout the book, Frost engages in generous and critical conversation with her Orthodox tradition, which she sees both as a deep well of wisdom and a work in progress. She does not shy away from grappling with the "not so wonderful parts of the tradition." Yet she finds that Orthodox incarnational theology offers significant resources for renewal. In some cases, faithful laypeople are already re-creating the tradition anew with ritual adaptations and new prayers. In other cases, Frost hopes that theologian-mothers will have a voice in rethinking practices and ways of thinking that have strayed from the best Christian insights.

At several points, Frost speaks of her project as a kind of "theology of the body." In my own Catholic tradition, this term is highly charged. For some it represents profound thinking about how bodies reveal truths about human existence and the moral life. For others, it is a dangerously narrow sexual ethic, lacking the very incarnational perspective it claims to hold. Frost's theology of the body cuts right through those divisions and invites broad engagement. Her theology of the body involves reflecting theologically on the embodied experiences of motherhood that are central to the Christian tradition and the lives of mothers. It means taking readers through the stages of conception, pregnancy, birth, postpartum, nursing, and weaning, and offering fresh insights about Christian life. For mothers and other believers who are open to seeing the sacred in the ordinary, this wonderful book provides insight into little-known parts of the Christian tradition and encourages new ways of seeing everyday life through the lens of faith.

Julie Hanlon Rubio
Jesuit School of Theology of Santa Clara
Berkeley, California

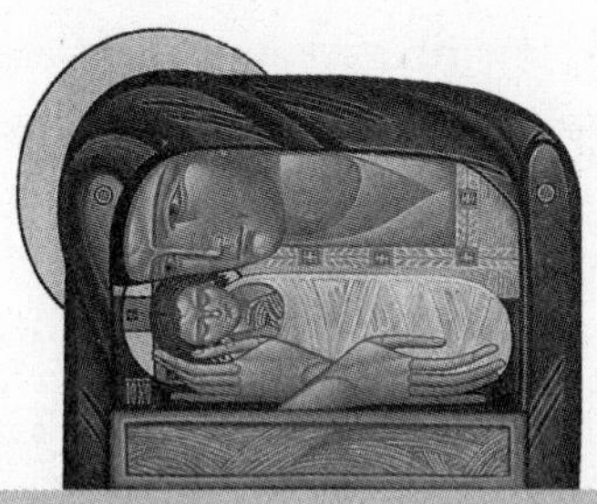

PREFACE

The maternal body is essential to our existence, every one of us. We each make our appearance in the cosmos through a maternal body. Our mother's body gives us our own body. In these bodies we live our lives and find our way into the next. A particular mother's body—Mary's—is fundamental to our existence as Christians. Jesus Christ became incarnate in the cosmos, the very cosmos he fashioned, through his mother's body. Mary's maternal body gave him his body, in which he grew, taught, was crucified, conquered death, and was resurrected. The maternal body holds cosmic and eternal significance, and offers insight into our own, embodied human existence.

About a decade ago I found myself pregnant with triplets halfway through work on a PhD in theology at the University of Virginia. My husband and I had thought long and hard about having a third child, so the joke was on us when, to our total surprise, we learned at a routine ultrasound that I was carrying not just our third child, but also our fourth and fifth!

Each of our family members had a different reaction to the news. My memory of that afternoon includes my husband uncharacteristically bouncing up and down in the ultrasound room, all glee. When we told our six-year-old daughter, who had been lobbying for a younger sibling since she herself was more or less a baby, she climbed up onto the dining room table and sobbed with happiness. Our oldest son, then eight and more reserved in nature, was silent for a moment and then observed, "We're going to need a bigger house."

My reaction? I wrote this book.

Of course, that is a long story made short. Initially I was daunted. I knew that my pregnancy was now high risk, with the specter of complications, and that premature delivery with its concomitant problems for newborns was likely. At the same time, I was delighted. After all our hand-wringing over whether to have another child, the astonishing reality of triplets came as an unalloyed affirmation of my vocation as a mother.

Ultimately, my triplet pregnancy truly did lead me to write this book. I had been a mother for nearly eight years by that point, and I had occasionally sought theological reflection on motherhood over those years, but the intensity of impending infants in triplicate gave new urgency to this quest.

I was readily aware of the rich imagery of motherhood in my own tradition, Orthodox Christianity. Simply by setting foot in an Orthodox Church, a person is overwhelmed by images of maternity: images of Mary holding her infant son Jesus abound alongside icons that celebrate the conception and birth of particular saints, such as Mary herself and John the Baptist. Words in praise of Mary's motherhood are often heard, as in the eucharistic prayers: "It is truly right to bless you, Theotokos [Greek for "Birthgiver of God"], ever blessed, most pure, and Mother of our God."[1] With all these marvelous treatments of motherhood available, I assumed there were complementary theological treatises.

But this was not so. Despite all the imagery and hymnic praise of mothers that is part of everyday church life, motherhood is not a topic that has been taken up for deep theological reflection in the Orthodox tradition. Thus, I set out to tap Orthodox sources—icons, feasts, and prayers—for theological information about motherhood, and this book is the result. Though some of the Orthodox sources on motherhood are held in common with my Protestant and Catholic sisters and brothers, I have found them to be largely unknown outside of Orthodoxy and often unappreciated and unexamined within Orthodoxy, so I take care to orient my reader along the way.

At the outset of my work, I expected to find affirmations of motherhood, since that was what I was seeing on the walls around me at church and hearing during liturgy, and since motherhood was viewed favorably in my church experience. I did find some affirmation, but I found other, more complex portrayals of motherhood as well. Most interesting to me, I found an understanding of motherhood in which spirituality and physicality are deeply intertwined, which affirmed my own experience of motherhood—of my own *maternal body*.

For me, motherhood is ferociously physical. My march through the initial biological process of motherhood—conception, pregnancy, childbirth, the postpartum time, and breastfeeding—was full of palpable, material changes to my physical being. More than that, and beyond that time of early motherhood, are the ways in which motherhood anchors my attention in my own skin, in my body. No longer was I able to live largely in the abstractions of the mind; my existence was newly moored in my physical being when I became a mother, moored in my own maternal body. This experience was echoed by other mothers around me, and not just biological mothers; my friends who adopted children also experienced the anchor of the maternal body.

I furthermore encountered depictions of motherhood in Orthodoxy that did *not* affirm motherhood as a vocation and did *not* affirm the maternal body. In fact, I found times when my tradition denigrates the maternal body, contrary to its deep reverence for the human form based on the incarnation. Encountering these disparities having to do with motherhood, and especially with the maternal body, prompted me to reckon with the ways in which the church has failed to live up to its theology of the body. Discomfort with parts of one's tradition is hardly an experience unique to me, particular to motherhood, or confined to the Orthodox context; it is shared with people belonging to ancient churches and faiths. We also share the need for ways of encountering the imperfect record of our traditions, and I reflect on this challenge throughout this book.

Orthodox icons, prayers, and feasts; the vivid embodied experience of motherhood; and the disquiet caused by dissonant practices and ideas in the church—I invite my reader to consider all of these things with me throughout *Maternal Body*.

Searching for Mothers in the Fathers

As I looked for sources on motherhood, I began to ponder why, even in a tradition that is founded on an act of motherhood and contains so many images of motherhood in its icons and hymns, there is so little written theological reflection on this topic. The key reason is very straightforward: the Christian theological landscape has been absolutely dominated by men. Those inclined to write about motherhood would be, naturally, mothers; and women, much less mothers, have not been theologians in my tradition. I like to joke that I went "searching for mothers in the Fathers"—the patristic thinkers of the early Christian church—clearly a futile quest. Every now and again, I hear someone say, "The church fathers *and the church mothers*," usually in an earnest and well-meaning reference to some of the early desert-dwelling female monastics, from whom we do have some writings. Rarely can someone who references the church mothers in this way actually name one—this is just good-intentioned ahistorical tokenism. The "church mothers" simply did not form the church's theology like the fathers.

In addition to all being men, most of the church fathers lived celibate lives, having left their own mothers behind at a young age, and many of them lived in monasteries with little or no contact with women. Some quite openly devalued motherhood; for example, Saint Jerome praised fifth-century Saint Paula for sailing away to become a nun while her abandoned young son cried on the shore.[2] Even the vast majority of patristic writings on the church's most visible mother, Mary, were focused not on her motherhood but instead on her virginity, which accorded better with the Christian way of life that the church fathers themselves embraced.

The historical dominance of the male perspective in Christianity extends beyond celibate monastics and well past the patristic era; men have accounted for the vast majority of lay theologians and, of course, all the married clergy theologians, as well as nearly all the iconographers and hymnographers throughout Christian history. Because until the last century or so, and only now with some Protestant exceptions, men are exclusively the priests or pastors in Christian churches, women have rarely had the opportunity to receive theological training. The rare exceptions arise from remarkable circumstances, such as Sister Madeleva Wolff's founding of the first graduate theology school open to women at St. Mary's College in Notre Dame in the 1940s. Notably, there is no parallel Orthodox institution, though there are examples of erudite women's monasteries. All this is to say that, though there has never been a formal ban on women theologians, the effect of the male-managed, celibate-focused Christian theological conversation has been much the same: a relatively small proportion of theological reflection of any type has been generated by women in the two-thousand-year history of Christianity.

The absence of women theologians is of particular note in the Orthodox Church compared to other Christian churches; it is a statement of fact that women have only rarely participated in theological discussions or contributed to the written record of theological reflection in Orthodoxy. In contrast to our Western Christian sisters, we do not even have exceptions that prove the rule; we have no parallel examples to Catherine of Siena, Julian of Norwich, Margery Kempe, or Hildegard of Bingen, and others who managed—one way or another—to claim a space for their own theological voices. There are women of significance in Orthodox history, including intellectuals, such as Saint Catherine of Alexandria of the fourth century; travelogue writers, such as Egeria, also of the fourth century; and icon defenders, such as Byzantine Empress Theodora of the ninth century. Each of these women contributed to Orthodoxy in her way, but none was a theologian per se.

The twentieth century produced two Orthodox women theologians whose prominence has grown with time: Elisabeth Behr-Sigel and Saint Mother Maria Skobtsova, both mothers (even though, as her name notes, the latter became a nun later in life), and this is evidence that the tide is beginning to turn. There also seems to be church-wide interest in matters of women and family; Pope Francis has, on several occasions, called for a "theology of women."[3] Women are now being theologically trained in meaningful numbers in a variety of Christian traditions, and are becoming theologians, scholars, even professors teaching male seminarians, and this is even the case in the Orthodox Church.

It seems that the church that declared in the fourth century, in the words of Saint Basil, that the natures of men and women are "alike of equal honor, the virtues...equal, the struggle equal, the judgment alike,"[4] only now is beginning to appreciate its women's theological voices as "alike in honor," too. I pause at several moments in *Maternal Body* to reflect on the future of Christian theology, and specifically Orthodox theology, now that women are joining the theological conversation.

On a personal note, the dearth of women theologians in my tradition makes me especially appreciative of my own situation—my guess is that there are no more than a few hundred Orthodox women in history who have received high-level theological training. Let me be clear: this does not automatically make me a good theologian, or one that has the final say on women and the church. Instead, I am simply appreciative of the good fortune that has allowed me to join their ranks and now work within the theological tradition of my church. I grew up as the second-generation descendant of Russians who came to the United States for work in the early twentieth century, attending a tiny Orthodox parish in the coalfields of West Virginia. It was there that I asked my first questions about women in the church, which were given unsatisfying answers when answered at all. To be now in a position to work toward answering those questions is humbling, daunting, and nothing short of amazing to me.

The Orthodox Sources

In line with my expectations, I found many unmined sources on motherhood within Orthodoxy. I found icons that depict every stage in the process of biological motherhood, which are featured throughout the book. I knew that Saint John Chrysostom, bishop and famous homilist of the fourth century, was one of the few thinkers from the patristic era to reflect on family at any length, and I also found that he dedicated thought here and there to motherhood specifically. In perusing Orthodox hymnography, I found that Saint Ephrem the Syrian was moved to praise Mary's maternal body at many points in the hymns he composed—some of which were composed exclusively for female choirs—and that sixth-century Saint Romanos the Melodist wrote hymns about her maternity, too. I so enjoyed exploring all these sources.

However, part of the process of working with these wonderful sources on the maternal body was encountering some not-so-wonderful sources that are also part of my Orthodox tradition. For example, in the late Byzantine period, for various reasons, the idea that childbirth made a woman "impure" was introduced into the churching prayers that welcome a new mother back to church after having a baby. In the Christian West, there were parallel prayers, but they fell into disuse, whereas the churching prayers are used to this day in the Orthodox Church—histories on which I will elaborate in chapter 4. Given that impurity has long been equated with sin in Christianity, these prayers have been spiritually harmful for hundreds of years by conveying to women that their birthgiving is sinful. Sources such as this were hard for me to reckon with.

But, I chose not to shy away from the moments when the church strays from its truths. Some friends encouraged me to "showcase Orthodoxy," and one suggested I ought to produce a "beautiful coffee table book." I love my church and I believe that it offers a rich vision of the maternal body, but this is no coffee table book. For one thing, I cannot abide the intellectual dishonesty it would require for me to only highlight the "good" sources from my tradition, only the sources that support a positive view of motherhood. For another, the more I worked with the material for this book, the more I personally had to come to terms with the ways in which my own beloved church is imperfect—and particularly imperfect when it comes to mothers' bodies—and the more I realized that it would behoove all of us Christians today to encounter more honestly the failings of our communities; this is an issue much larger than my book.

Within Orthodoxy, for example, we are often loath to criticize our venerable tradition. We are quick to judge "the world"—as defined as everything outside the church—harshly, but hesitant to be clear-eyed in our evaluation of the church. One of our obstacles to seeing our community clearly is our understanding of the church as the "mystical body of Christ," made of baptized members, past and present, united in the Eucharist throughout time. This is a beautiful theological truth that is integral to the self-identity of the Orthodox

Church. However, when the Orthodox Church thinks of itself *only* in this way, and forgets—or denies—that it is, at any one moment in chronological time, also composed of imperfect humans living in a fallen state, then it fails to encounter the ways in which it is itself a fallen body. When the church perceives itself as perfect, there is no model for how to acknowledge its failures, much less how to overcome them. This challenge is not unique to Orthodoxy; it is also faced by other churches that understand themselves similarly.

Another stumbling block to encountering our imperfections is our allegiance to tradition in contrast to the rapidly changing modern world. I am certainly not the first person to grapple with how to live within an "ancient faith in modern times," but I see much of the talk around this in Orthodox circles—and in Catholic circles as well—as having to do with either a certain pride in the longevity of our attention span in contrast to the world around us (e.g., "We are still serving a sixteen-hundred-year-old liturgy in the age of the internet!"), or hostility to the world today (e.g., "The church is bastion of righteousness under siege from various, nefarious threats of secular society!"). Instead, I understand living one's ancient faith today as having to do with the work of fully engaging with one's tradition, flaws and all, not just favorably contrasting it to the world.

This is not to say that the view from the early twenty-first century is an objective one from which all imperfections of the Christian tradition can be named and remedied; we moderns are just as mired in our own subjectivity as anyone from any other period. We do, however, have the benefit, when it comes to this particular topic, of women theologians today and of *actual mothers* now writing about motherhood, and these are authentically objective improvements in perspective.

This process of encountering the imperfections in my own tradition was enormously helpful to me in my own spiritual life. I have had many difficult moments in the church: everything from encounters with bad theology from the pulpit, to an abusive confessor, to being called a heretic for my work on women and the church, and more. All these experiences generated discord within me.

My work on *Maternal Body*, however, allowed me to accept some of my internal discord and recognize that the church, in its human expression, is flawed, imperfect, and sometimes wrong when it comes to mothers' bodies. And, more importantly, my work on *Maternal Body* allowed me to see that it is the vocation of Christian faithful, like myself, who love their church, to work to rectify its flaws, to right any wrongs, and to bring the church to perfection—as much as is possible in this life.

A Theology of the Body

In addition to providing reflection on motherhood and the imperfections of the church, the Orthodox sources on motherhood also lend themselves to much-needed reflection on our embodied human experience. Indeed, they are, in their fullness, a corrective to disparaging views of the body that surround and infect the church.

The Christian vision of the body is anything but disparaging. Christianity takes our bodily existence very seriously because our bodies are God-given, and especially because our God himself took on a body. As Saint Athanasius of the fourth century explains, Jesus Christ chose to enter the world in this manner: "He takes unto Himself a body, and that of no different sort from ours. For He did not simply will to become embodied, or will merely to appear. For if He willed merely to appear, He was able to effect His divine appearance by some other and higher means as well. But He takes a body of our kind."[5]

To take on a human body "of no different sort from ours" means that Jesus Christ experienced the same body that we experience: his mother gave him flesh in the womb, he was born as a vulnerable infant, his body grew in childhood, and it matured into its adult form and continued to change as the years passed, just as is the case for each of us. This was not happenstance, as second-century Saint Irenaeus expresses when describing Jesus and his incarnation: "...the only true and steadfast Teacher, the Word of God, our Lord Jesus Christ, who did, through His transcendent love, become what we are, that He might bring us to be even what He is Himself."[6] Jesus Christ became what we are so that we might become what he is. It is important to note here that the emphasis in Orthodox theology is entirely on Jesus Christ becoming *human*, not male. In no way is the possibility of becoming "what he is" qualified to just men.

The idea that humans are destined to become "what he is," to become like God—to experience "deification"—is central to the Orthodox Christian understanding of human life. Synonymous with "divinization" or *theosis*, the concept of deification is certainly present in, and accessible to, other Christian churches. This way of speaking about the vocation of humanity is the dominant one in Orthodoxy. *Deification* means "the process of becoming more like God, of drawing closer to God, of entering communion with God." There is a way in which this is a return to our true selves; we were made in the "image and likeness" of God, we tarnished that, and through our deification, we, with God's grace, return to communion with our creator.

Deification is not a gnostic process that takes place on a spiritual plane, nor an academic one that takes place in the mind. The spirit and the mind are involved, to be sure, but their workshop is the body. Jesus Christ, through his own incarnation, brings us to be "even what he is himself" through our own incarnation: this is the Orthodox Christian theology of the body, the church's incarnational theology, in a nutshell. I find this to be an endlessly fascinating point of the Christian story: God became human, became embodied, in order to experience a new intimacy with us, so that we might experience a new intimacy with him—within our bodies, which are now blessed afresh by his incarnation.

As noted, though, the church's historical record has not been perfect on this point—it has sometimes expressed disparaging views of the human body, and, unfortunately, especially of women's bodies and of mothers' bodies—as I will address at several moments in *Maternal Body*. Furthermore, there are also disparaging understandings of the body that are threatening our incarnational theology today. Our larger culture outside the church, on the one hand, worships the body, in the sense that there is no end to the emphasis placed on looking good (especially for women) and on products and procedures that ought to be acquired to support such efforts. On the other hand, the larger culture denigrates the body in that so many aspects of modern living work against the well-being of the body: excessive use of electronic screens, long hours sitting, not sleeping enough, driving everywhere rather than walking, and so on. In these ways, modern life is very disembodied. We are trained either not to accept our bodies as they are but to always seek to change them, or to ignore our bodies entirely.

The Orthodox sources on motherhood often affirm the goodness of the human body by depicting with reverence and care various stages of physical maternity. For example, chapter 2 includes an icon of the Visitation, of Mary and Elizabeth visiting each other and embracing each other while both pregnant—their maternal bodies are apparent and treated with honor. But, there are also times, as noted, when the sources are out of alignment with the church's profound incarnational theology, and in those cases I work to show how the church's presentation of the maternal body and its theology of the incarnation can be beautifully harmonized. When they are in tune, they—along with the corporeal reality of the maternal body—offer a new, fresh way of contemplating our incarnation, and serve as a corrective to distorted notions about the body both inside and outside the church.

Maternal Body

Each chapter is centered around one part of the biological process of motherhood. I, first, describe the biological happenings during that stage in order to firmly ground my reader in the lived, corporeal experience of motherhood. I also share some of my own stories, not because I think them exceptional, but because I wish to underscore that this work on motherhood comes from me, personally—that my thoughts on motherhood are shaped by my own physical experience of it.

I, then, examine a source or two that elucidates a biological stage of the maternal body. The icon of Joachim and Anna, Mary's parents, poised in front of their marital bed just before they conceive, is the focus of chapter 1: Conception. In this chapter, I also lament certain ways the Orthodox Church has treated cases of infertility or miscarriage. Moreover, I illustrate that the image and the story of Joachim and Anna affirm the goodness of marital sexuality and lay the groundwork for a consideration of the maternal body. In chapter 2: Pregnancy, I consider the importance of the maternal body to the existence of Orthodox icons in general, and then admire an Annunciation icon and a Visitation icon that depict the pregnant forms of the saints therein, quite literally showing the Orthodox Church's regard for the pregnant maternal body. I also consider the changes in depictions of female saints taking place within the bounds of traditional, canonical iconography today, as more women and mothers become iconographers than ever before.

Mary's appearance as the first Christian contemplative—just after giving birth, no less—as shown in the Nativity icon is the focus of chapter 3: Birthgiving. Here I also consider the ways in which Mary's maternal body is portrayed in different styles of Nativity icons and what this says about the church's views of her maternal body. Mentioned earlier, churching, the ritual for welcoming mothers back to church after childbirth, with its many deficiencies and many possibilities, is examined in chapter 4: Postpartum. I attend to the history of the connection between impurity and childbirth in the prayers and discuss how they are changing today and how they might best be reconsidered, both to maintain their hospitality to the new mother and also to reflect the church's teachings on the goodness of the human body, especially the maternal body. In chapter 5: Breastfeeding, I look at images that show Mary nursing Christ, images that, though never common in the Christian East, maintained a persistent presence throughout Christian time and place. I consider the way Mary's maternal body is depicted in these images and consider this depiction in light of the church's theology of the body. In the epilogue, I contemplate the significance of the maternal body for the life of a mother and the significance of the maternal body for the life of the church, and I look hopefully to the future of the church, as more mothers join its theological tradition.

At many points, I invoke the Mother of God, Mary, and her experience of motherhood. I do so aware that often her virginal body is celebrated above, and even to the neglect of, her maternal body; she is frequently presented as more incorporeal angel than embodied human. And yet we hear from Scripture and tradition that Mary was pregnant with Jesus, gave birth to him, nursed him, bathed him, and took care of him. Mary's maternal body was elemental to Jesus Christ's incarnation, and I contend that it holds great meaning for how we ought to understand our own bodies. Her body and, truly, all maternal bodies uniquely protect a Christian vision of the human body as Creator-fashioned, integral to salvation, and destined for eternity—a vision that is vital not just for mothers, but all humans.

The maternal body is also uniquely evocative of incarnational theology because the experience of motherhood is expressly embodied. I have allowed the process of biological motherhood to determine the shape of the book for the sake of employing fresh theological categories, but also precisely for this reason, to underscore the incessant corporeal reality of motherhood with the very evocative physical images of conception, pregnancy, and so forth. Even so, while the corporeal experience of biological motherhood plays out differently than that of adoptive motherhood, motherhood is always ineluctably physical. No matter what age or circumstance in which a woman becomes a mother, there is no shortage of maternal physicality and maternal care for her child and herself.

The physicality of motherhood of a pregnant teenager may be quite different from that of the maternal body of a grandmother who unexpectedly finds that she must raise a grandchild. A married, adoptive mother's maternal body may experience other changes and sensations than those of a single, biological mother. Even with their different maternal experiences, each of these mothers has her own maternal body. The changes a mother experiences in her maternal body over time and the physical intimacy of caring for another are so conspicuous and so definitional of everyday experience as a mother that they cannot be ignored. A mother must sink into her own body, she must grapple with its changes, she is forced to experience the aches and pains and the pleasures and joys of being drawn down into her embodied being every day.

We all need to be drawn into our embodied beings. Not only are there so many temptations that pull us away—screens, newsfeeds, other demands of modern life—but the consequences of living as though disembodied are tragic: we take care neither of ourselves, nor of creation. We need to be fully embodied in order to be our true selves, in deep relationship with each other, the world, and the church. We need to embrace our incarnation in order to experience deification. The maternal body leads us into our bodies, so that there we can find God. May this book do so also.

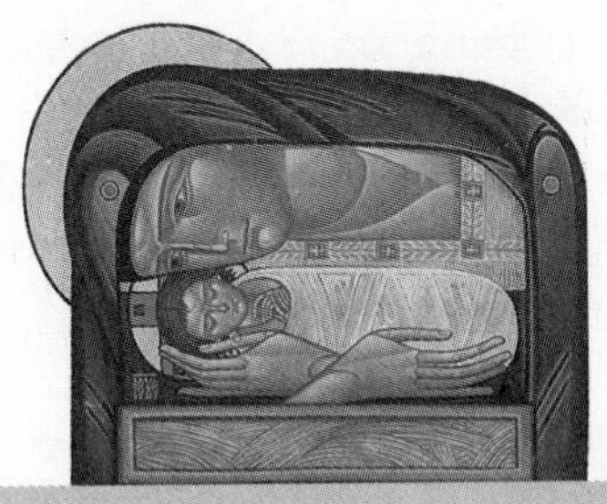

ACKNOWLEDGMENTS

The unflagging encouragement and generous advice of Wes Hill, Veronica Mary Rolf, and Bria Sanford were essential to this book making it to print; thank you. I thank Trace Murphy for bringing me into the Paulist fold and my editor there, Nancy de Flon, for her keen work and efficacious manner.

I thank the dozens of people who have helped me, in one way or another, in my work on motherhood over the years, and among those I offer particular gratitude to Tom Tiller, Rebecca Rine, Presbytera Elizabeth Tervo, Marilyn Rouvelas, Pamela Wright, Emily Schulte, Father Robert Holet, and my mentor and friend, Vigen Guroian. I specifically thank my friends and colleagues who read portions of this book or talked through aspects of it with me over the years: Jenni Malyon, Matt Malyon, Jana Schofield, Mary Cunningham, Nina Glibetic, Carolyn McCarthy, Alexandra Schmalzbach, and Holly Loth; and others who helped me find icons and translate icon epithets: Matt Crutchmer and Ivan Plis.

Most of all, I thank my family. I thank my husband, Matt, for having the best idea ever to enter into the "indissoluble bond of love" of marriage with me and create a family together. And I thank those to whom I owe my maternal body, my children: Cyrus, Ann, Eliza, Beatrix, and Ignatius. Thank you, and I love you.

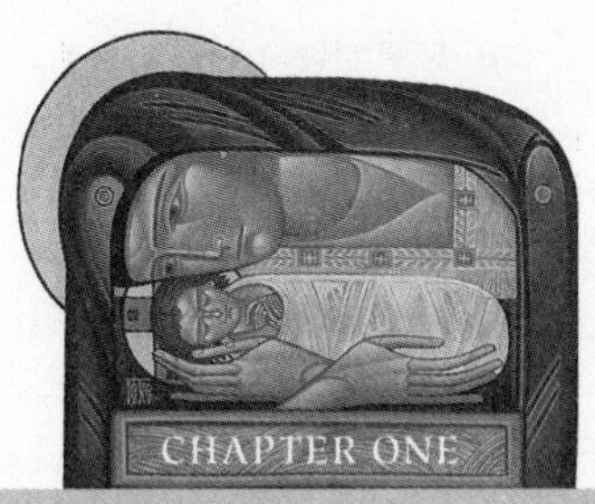

CONCEPTION

In Orthodox Christian thinking, conception is understood as the advent of a new person, a result of the sexual union of his or her parents as well as of the grace of God. This is different from, but not mutually exclusive with, the approach to human conception taught in high school health class, where conception is understood as just the union of an ovum from a woman and a spermatozoon from a man.

In Orthodoxy, the emphasis is placed not on the biological precision of the fusion of cells, but on the person created in divine-human partnership. That is why one is hard-pressed to find an Orthodox definition of when life technically begins in utero. The divine participation in conception is recalled by the prophet Jeremiah when he speaks of God's acquaintance with each person before birth: "Before I formed you in the womb I knew you, and before you were born I consecrated you" (Jer 1:5). That each new human person is known and blessed by God from the beginning of her or his formation is integral to an Orthodox perspective on conception, and, truly, on the human person.

This appreciation for the formation of a new person adds to the reasons a woman who hopes to be a mother might look forward to conceptive union with her husband. In the Orthodox tradition, marriage is typically expected to be, at least for a portion of its history, open to childbearing—barring mental or physical constraints and often with contraception judiciously and prayerfully employed. It is important to note here that an Orthodox marriage that is unable to create children is in no way a diminished union. As Saint John Chrysostom of the fourth century writes, "But suppose there is no child; do they [the married couple] remain two and not one? No; their intercourse effects the joining of their bodies, and they are made one, just as when perfume is mixed with ointment."[1] This stance is an extension of the theological and ethical vision of marriage in Orthodoxy, which understands children as an important part of the unitive quality of marriage, but not as a definitive characteristic of marriage.

After uniting with her husband, a woman who is seeking to conceive remains hopeful in the time between then and the detection of a pregnancy a couple of weeks later. However, there is no promise that conceptive efforts will result in a pregnancy, or that a pregnancy will go smoothly. My own experiences echo the unpredictability of this part of motherhood. I worried that health problems might compromise my ability to conceive. I also experienced one suspected but unverified early miscarriage, a minor-order surprise pregnancy with my second child, and—of all the shocking things ever to happen to an expectant mother—news of a triplet pregnancy at the end of a first trimester—news that meant our family would grow overnight from four people to seven. I will not soon forget the ultrasound technician saying in a singsong voice, "I have a surprise for you!"

Conception

The news of that pregnancy just got more shocking after birth when we had reason to further ponder the particulars of their conception. Though the triplets had separate equipment in the womb (different sacs and placentas), which led us to believe that they were fraternal, they were actually one pair of identical girls with a fraternal brother. This only began to become apparent to us when, a few hours after their birth, my husband turned to me and solemnly said, "These girls look a lot alike." In our sleep-deprived state, we were never rational enough to come to terms with the obvious, so we used a cheek-swab DNA test to confirm that the girls are identical.

Just this morning at the breakfast table, the triplets, who are nine years old now, told me the story of their origins, which is a tale they love to tell and hear over and over again. The girls pantomime their cellular split by first joining hands in a big circle and then splitting into two circles formed by just their own hands, while their brother keeps his hands together in an unbroken circle the whole time. There is even a little theme song they hum, to narrate their telling of what took place soon after their conception that resulted in three persons from just two eggs. For me, my own tales of the beginnings of my children feel quite private. This is much to the disappointment of strangers, many of whom want to hear all the ins and outs of how I came to carry triplets.

In contrast, tales of conception in my Orthodox Christian tradition are told openly and unabashedly. The conceptions of Jesus Christ and various saints—even with clear reference to the sexual union of the parents—are given quite public treatment in the Orthodox Church, in its hymns, images, and feasts. In fact, three feasts of conception are included in the high days of the church: the Annunciation

(Mary's exceptional conception of her son, Jesus Christ), the Conception of Anna, sometimes called the Conception of the Mother of God (Saints Anna and Joachim's conception of their daughter, Mary herself), and the Conception of Saint John the Baptist (Saints Elizabeth and Zechariah's conception of their son, John). Images for these feasts appear in nearly every Orthodox church, often in places of prominence; the Annunciation icon is typically front and center on the altar doors. The services associated with these feasts are replete with hymns celebrating these conceptions. For example, on the Feast of the Conception of Saint John, we sing

> Great Zachariah rejoices with his wife, the far-
> famed Elizabeth,
> for she has fittingly conceived John the
> Forerunner,
> whom an angel announced in gladness;
> and whom we rightly honor
> as an initiate of the grace of God.[2]

Stories of two of these conceptions come from the New Testament—the Annunciation (Luke 1:26–39) and the Conception of John (Luke 1:5–25)—and are preceded in Scripture by typological tales of other miraculous or improbable conceptions, including the Old Testament stories of Sarah, Rebekah, Rachel, Leah, Sampson's mother, and Hannah. These holy conceptions are also openly referred to in the Orthodox marriage rite—often jokingly referred to as the "Orthodox fertility rite" because of the frequency of its childbearing references—when the following words are prayed: "Thou didst bless Thy servant Abraham, and opening the womb of Sarah didst make him to be the father of many nations. Thou didst give Isaac to Rebecca, and didst bless her in child bearing. Thou didst join Jacob unto Rachel...."[3] While the tale of Anna's conception of Mary is not preserved in Scripture, it is firmly ensconced in Orthodox tradition, on which I will elaborate later.

This chapter has my special affection because Anna is my own saint; my middle name is "Ann" after my Russian paternal grandmother. I was most enamored with Saint Anna's epithet as a small child: *Ancestor of God*. To me that sounded almost better than God himself. Now, as an adult immersed in sources on motherhood in the church, I see that Saint Anna can also be considered the ancestor of the Orthodox appreciation for the maternal body.

While this chapter is dedicated to the inherent esteem of marital conjugality in the Orthodox sources, I also reflect on Orthodox understandings of situations in which conception does not go as hoped—cases of infertility and miscarriage. I do so to honor these realities in the pursuit of motherhood. I do so also because these are cases where the Orthodox Church has failed to respond compassionately to women experiencing these realities. Here I expose a flaw in Orthodox tradition, a flaw that begins the thread of consideration about living within a venerable, magnificent, but imperfect tradition, a thread that is sewn throughout this book.

"Today the World Rejoices in the Conception of Anna"

Anyone who encounters a woman in late pregnancy sees that motherhood is a physical affair—her maternal body is visible to the world, it is public. The act of conception, though private, shares that physicality in two ways. Obviously, conception is precipitated by a physical act when the woman experiences sexual union with her husband. Second, in sexual union with her husband, she offers herself up to the physical experience of pregnancy and childbearing; she invites, with the grace of God, another human to share her body. This invitation constitutes the ultimate act of hospitality. In the Orthodox Church, this physical and ultimate act of hospitality is beautifully expressed in the story of Mary's own conception by her parents and the icon representing this conception.

The Feast of the Righteous Anna's Conception of the Mother of God is celebrated on December 9, and although it was included in the church calendar around the eighth century, stories of Anna's conception of Mary date to a much earlier time. The same event is celebrated on the Roman Catholic calendar a day earlier, December 8, as the Immaculate Conception, though the feast has a differing theological tone, given that the Catholic West came to understand Mary as unaffected by original sin from her conception, whereas the Christian East holds a different understanding of inherited sin altogether and does not understand Mary's immaculateness dogmatically. Anna's story comes not from the New Testament but from church tradition, which likely began as oral stories about Mary and her parents. These stories were then compiled and likely embellished in the second-century Christian document the *Protoevangelium of James*. As its title suggests, it is not one of the canonical Gospels, but contains information about events that precede ("proto") the Gospels' narrative of the life of Jesus Christ. The *Protoevangelium* is also called the *Book of James* because of its putative author, a title I use here.

Although the *Book of James* was never blessed as canonical Scripture, which is important to bear in mind, it must have scratched an itch for more information about Jesus Christ's beginnings and childhood because its popularity in the ancient world is undeniable, given the extant copies found in different languages, different places, and different time periods. The tales included in the *Book of James* are not considered by Orthodox to be historical and incontrovertible fact, but instead are understood as meaningful reflections on the life of Jesus and his mother.

For a book not understood to be incontrovertible fact, the *Book of James* is long on details. Unlike the canonical Gospels, the *Book of James* offers many minutiae of Mary's life, on the conception of her by her parents, her birth, and her upbringing. These details from the *Book of James* were enormously influential on the church's iconographic, hymnic, and homiletic depictions of Mary, the premier mother of the church. Truly, they must have been fabulous to read by early Christians who probably yearned for an intimate look at Jesus Christ's family of origin since this is a topic on which the Gospels are largely silent.

The *Book of James* starts with Mary's parents, Joachim and Anna, arriving in old age childless, to their great disappointment and public shame. It is hard for us today to imagine this sort of shame. Couples today who are without children may endure some questions and some teasing that will fall silent once they are past childbearing age. They may well experience some associated shame, but they will not be publicly disgraced. They will not be denied their right to worship, as was Joachim when he was told by a priest of the temple, "It is not meet for you first to bring your offerings, because you have not made seed in Israel." Unsurprisingly, Joachim was "exceedingly grieved."[4]

Anna was also grieved and is said to have "prayed to the Lord, saying: 'O God of our fathers, bless me and hear my prayer, as You blessed the womb of Sarah, and gave her a son Isaac.'"[5] The account of her prayer continues:

> And gazing towards the heaven, she saw a sparrow's nest in the laurel, and made lamentation in herself, saying: Alas! Who begot me? And what womb produced me? Because I have become a curse in the presence of the sons of Israel, and I have been reproached, and they have driven me in derision out of the temple of the Lord. Alas! To what have I been likened? I am not like the fowls of the heaven, because even the fowls of the heaven are productive before You, O Lord. Alas! To what have I been likened? I am not like the beasts of the earth, because even the beasts of the earth are productive before You, O Lord. Alas! To what have I been likened? I am not like these waters, because even these waters are productive before You, O Lord. Alas! To what have I been likened? I am not like this earth, because even the earth brings forth its fruits in season, and blesses You, O Lord.[6]

Anna's anguish is clear in this telling. Seeing motherhood before her in its avian form, Anna desires to share this experience with her fellow creatures, and it pains her that even the earth seems to procreate when she does not. The answer to Anna's prayer is swift and definitive: "And, behold, an angel of the Lord stood by, saying: 'Anna, Anna, the Lord has heard your prayer, and you shall conceive, and shall bring forth; and your seed shall be spoken of in all the world.'"[7] Anna replies, "As the Lord my God lives, if I beget either male or female, I will bring it as a gift to the Lord my God; and it shall minister to Him in holy things all the days of its life."[8] It is notable that within the context of a culture that valued sons over daughters, especially in reference to the first-born of a family, Anna explicitly expresses delight in either a prospective son *or* a daughter.

Joachim has also secluded himself in the natural world in prayer, and he also encounters a holy messenger who bears the news from God that his and Anna's sorrow will soon come to an end. After their angelic encounters, the two rush home to meet each other: "And, behold, Joachim came with his flocks; and Anna stood by the gate...and she ran and hung upon his neck, saying: 'Now I know that the Lord God has blessed me exceedingly; for, behold...I the childless shall conceive.' And Joachim rested the first day in his house."[9]

The phrase "rested in his house" intimates that Anna and Joachim unite sexually and conceive. Indeed, nine months later, Anna gives birth to Mary, the Mother of God. The Orthodox Church acknowledges and celebrates Anna's conception of Mary in song:

> Today the universe rejoices,
> For Anna has conceived the Theotokos through
> God's dispensation,
> For she has brought forth the one who is to bear
> the ineffable Word![10]

The Feast of the Conception of Anna, as presented in the *Book of James* and in Orthodox hymns, is a foundation for the esteem for married sexuality in Orthodoxy.

The regard for married sexuality and conception is visually depicted in the icon that honors the union of Anna and Joachim, *Joachim and Anna* (alternately called *The Conception of Anna*). One of the treasures of Orthodoxy is its imagery—the ancient tradition of creating depictions of the saints and feasts to inspire the faithful and connect them with the Divine, discussed in more detail in the next chapter. The image included here by contemporary American iconographer Father Luke Dingman is faithful to the ancient depiction of this feast, which dates back for at least a thousand years, though its basic configuration has remained the same over time (see Figure 1).

This icon illustrates the moment from the *Book of James* when Anna and Joachim rush to be together after each hearing from the angel that they will finally conceive a child. They are in such haste that their garments are aflutter, perhaps suggesting imminent removal. They intimately embrace; their arms are around each other, their faces are cheek-to-cheek. They look into one another's eyes, which is especially noteworthy since most icons depict saints looking either at the viewer or off to the side. Their shared gaze underscores that their marital intimacy is grace filled. As in this example, their marital bed is often conveniently positioned just behind them. In other examples, Orthodox iconographers sometimes borrow from the Western Christian tradition of the Golden Gate, based on the medieval *Golden Legend* composed by Jacobus Voragine in the thirteenth century, which told of Anna and Joachim meeting at the Golden Gate of the Old City in Jerusalem after each one's angelic encounter. Though they are shown in an embrace in this icon type as well, the ambiance is not quite as sensual without the bed at the ready. Nevertheless, all details in both types of *Joachim and Anna* icons point to Joachim and Anna's eagerness to unite sexually in order to create the child that they were promised.

No other icon so directly takes up the subject of sex. The sensual ambiance, including the couple's eagerness, conveys a sacramental notion of marital sex. The creation of a new person is shown to be a joyful event, possessing both spiritual and physical properties, that takes place in the context of a couple's affection. This is faithful to the Orthodox tradition in which sex is celebrated as a unitive act within marriage that bolsters the spiritual aspect of the "one flesh" partnership. A "conjugal being" is created, as Orthodox theologian Vigen Guroian eloquently calls it,[11] which well reflects representations of the married couple as one in Genesis (2:24), Ephesians (5:31), and the words of Jesus Christ (Matt 19:5–6; Mark 10:7–8). The conjugal being possible in marriage is beautifully represented in the *Joachim and Anna* icon.

This Orthodox insight about the one-flesh union, illustrated so well in the tale and icon of Anna's conception of Mary, also presents a vision of motherhood that embraces the physical aspect of conception—an affirmative beginning for an experience that is inescapably physical. The conjugal being is the theological genesis of motherhood in Orthodox thinking. The story and icon of Anna demonstrate that the body possesses its own grace in the context of sexuality in Christian marriage, and this grace extends to the woman as she begins her journey to motherhood. This icon is hanging, and not by accident, in my own marital bedroom.

"A Great Affliction": Infertility and Miscarriage

In addition to painting a lovely portrait of the experience of conception, Anna's story—given her long experience with infertility and her fervent prayers—also draws attention to the experience of women who long for children but have not conceived or who experience the loss of a pregnancy. These situations deserve reflection within the context of a consideration of motherhood.

When Anna struggled with barrenness, she took her struggle to God in prayer, and this act led to her conception of Mary. Her story, along with the many scriptural accounts of barren women turned fertile through prayer, seems fraught when applied to more pedestrian situations, because it prompts this question: How are women who are not the mother of a saint or prophet, or of anyone, to understand their own struggles with fertility in light of these scriptural stories of successful conceptions and pregnancies? I wrestled with this situation myself; although I ultimately gave birth to five children, I had several moments along the way when I wondered about my own ability to conceive. Like the mothers in Scripture, I took those fears and anxieties to God in prayer, but I certainly did not identify with their experience of divine intervention that led to a successful conception or count on a successful outcome based on their experience.

Saint John Chrysostom also grappled with these questions in his reflections on Hannah, the Old Testament mother of the prophet Samuel (1 Kgs 1) and one of Anna's sisters in infertility. Chrysostom addresses situations of women who wish to bear children but have not yet been able in light of the experience of Hannah, who, after her own period of infertility, went to the temple in fervent prayer and soon conceived her son.

Before I cite Chrysostom's thoughts on infertility, I will acknowledge that his inclusion in this book will immediately please some—many of his wonderfully pastoral homilies are translated into English and are being widely read, and there is a growing sentimental attachment to him in some Orthodox circles—but will immediately raise eyebrows in others, given that he is regarded in some Christian quarters as a hyperbolic misogynist, to put it lightly. It seems that he evokes either sentimental loyalty or hostility.

I would ask the former camp to recall his humanity when reading his thoughts on infertility below, which may surprise them, and perhaps to brace themselves for my (respectful) criticism of his thinking. I would ask the latter to remember that Chrysostom dedicates more thought to family and parenthood than any other theologian or homilist from the ancient Christian world, and he holds families and parents in high esteem. Flawed though some of his comments on women are, he elevates parenthood, and particularly motherhood, to a level of spiritual—not just pragmatic—importance, and for this reason he is a valuable interlocutor for this book.

Chrysostom is not unsympathetic to the burden of barrenness that Hannah experienced; he even takes the time to consider the social implications of her barrenness in her own time: "Think of how great an affliction the matter was considered in those days when…being barren and childless was a sort of curse and a death sentence."[12] Here is one of many places in which Chrysostom exhibits a sensitivity for family life uncommon among the early church thinkers.

Yet, even with his sympathy for those who experience infertility, Chrysostom extrapolates advice from Hannah's exceptional experience for the general population of women who are infertile—advice that I find difficult. For example, he suggests that by familiarizing themselves with Hannah's story, "childless women will be able to learn how to become mothers."[13] He elaborates: "If you come to him [the priest] with these [tears, prayers, and faith like Hannah's], you will receive all that you ask, and will go off in complete happiness."[14] Chrysostom concludes that it is Hannah's faith and fervor that results in a son, and that similar fervor on the part of other infertile women will produce the same results.

Chrysostom links fervor and fertility. This line of thinking is worrisome to me because it is just not the case—many women who fervently pray do not conceive. This thinking also promotes a sort of transactional understanding of prayer, which constitutes a sort of wishful thinking alien to the serious practice of prayer within Orthodoxy, but nevertheless present in some places today. For example, I know of Orthodox women trying to conceive who were offered dubious but well-intentioned formulas, such as "Make thirty-three prostrations in front of this icon once a day for forty days, and then you'll get pregnant."

Orthodoxy does indeed have a long tradition of miracle-working icons, prayers, and relics that are believed to assist fertility. One such item commonly referred to today is a purported piece of a garment of Mary's kept at the Vatopedi Monastery in the locus of male Orthodox monasticism: the peninsula full of monasteries in northern Greece called Mount Athos. Although, ironically, women are allowed neither at this monastery nor anywhere on Mount Athos, the monks there bless special ribbons near the relic and then send them all over the world to women who are seeking to get pregnant. Though traditions like Vatopedi ribbons may border on the transactional, or cross that line, many of these traditions simply acknowledge that the biological process of procreation alone does not make a new person; God is also involved.

The scriptural record on prayer and infertility is both inspiring and vexing: How does a woman seeking a child know when to persist in prayer, as did Hannah and Anna—or, in some cases, to persist in infertility treatments—and how does she know when to accept that she will not become a (biological) mother?

While I have no good answers for these questions, I find it helpful to return to a Christian vision of things that acknowledges that neither a child nor infertility is *deserved*—whether a couple conceives or is unable to do so, neither outcome is merited. This understanding is illustrated beautifully in the great Norwegian historical epic *Kristin Lavransdatter* (which, by the way, is the only work of world literature I know of that thoroughly revolves around the experience of motherhood) by Sigrid Undset, who two years after its completion became a Catholic. The eponymous character experiences a moment as a young Christian mother when the unwarranted wonder of motherhood hits her. She gazes down at her firstborn and reflects on how preposterously unfair it is that she, a flawed human, should have borne a creature of her own flesh that is "so pure, so healthy, so inexpressibly lovely. This undeserved beneficence broke her heart in two."[15] This literary example illustrates a Christian understanding of attempts to conceive a child: that just as no mother deserves to bear such a wonderful creature of her own flesh—her "underserved beneficence"—so also the fate of not being able to bear children is equally undeserved.

Another undeserved outcome of attempts to conceive is miscarriage, the loss of a known pregnancy that is thought to occur in at least 20 percent of pregnancies. Here a rift between Orthodox theology and Orthodox practice occurs. Although Orthodoxy has a sophisticated theology of life after death, and beautiful funeral rites and prayers for the dead, it has not always offered proper consolation on the occasion of the demise of the unborn. A chilling example is the service for miscarriage.

The rite is called "Prayer for a Woman When She Has Miscarried/Aborted an Infant." At first reading, the slash between "Miscarried" and "Aborted" might lead one to surmise that two different rites are contained therein: one for unintended pregnancy loss, and the other for cases of intended pregnancy loss (abortion). But, this is not the case. Both unintended and intended pregnancy loss are lumped together as one event for which the mother is deemed responsible. One prayer includes the line: "Have mercy on this Thy handmaid who today is in sin, having fallen into *the killing of a person*, whether voluntary or involuntary, and has cast out that conceived in her"[16] (italics not my own).

Understood in one light, this prayer is remarkably enlightened and generous, though this may not be immediately obvious. In the circumstance of an abortion, the "Prayer for a Woman When She Has Miscarried/Aborted an Infant" provides a means of reconciliation with the church. From its earliest days, the church has decried abortion, given its understanding of the human person's origins in the womb. This rite provides a way of peace and healing for women who have had an abortion, and it is a valuable reminder that the Orthodox Church includes a path for love and forgiveness, no matter what one's deeds. Although, I must note, as a theologian I cannot accept the use of the word *murderess*. Considering that women who abort often do so under extreme duress and coercion, I am unconvinced that the word *murderess* is theologically correct or pastorally helpful.

In the case of miscarriage, this prayer is the opposite of enlightened and generous. It is abominable because it places the responsibility for the demise of the unborn child, described as a "murder," on the mother. Some women who experience miscarriage have feelings of guilt, even though they are not at fault, and a generous reading of the "Prayer for a Woman When She Has Miscarried/Aborted an Infant" might suggest that it serves to cover this base. Clearly, though, there are ways to pray for a woman's unwarranted feelings of guilt or responsibility without labeling her as a "murderess."

The conflation of miscarriage with abortion may be a result of some historical confusion around what was a natural miscarriage versus an intended abortion, given that until only recently in Christendom it was thought that miscarriage was caused by eating certain foods or engaging in certain activities that are now understood to be unconnected to miscarriage. Still, the implication of this rite in its own time is clear: no one—perhaps especially the church and her parish priest—took a woman's self-proclamation about the loss of her pregnancy on faith.

Interestingly, the Orthodox miscarriage rite is a relatively new rite—"new" in the sense that it is only five hundred years or so old, which is young in Orthodox liturgical terms. The point is that most Orthodox rites were already ensconced in tradition when this rite was added to the books. Today, it is not often used in the American situation, and with good reason. In fact, American practice is highly variable in terms of rites of miscarriage and what pastoral care priests offer to the bereaved parents. I think of my own mother, whose first child was stillborn at full term. When she called the priest, he said, "There is nothing I can do for you," and did not so much as visit her in the hospital. Though being told "there is nothing I can do for you" may be a step up from being told one is a "murderess," this treatment deeply wounded her relationship with the church. Interestingly, when this priest retired decades after my brother's fleeting life, he called my mother and told her that not coming to her side was one of the biggest regrets of his priesthood. My mother was not alone in this experience—many women have had similar problems in the Orthodox Church, and in other Christian churches—this is an area in which many Christian communities stand to do better.

Engaging with Tradition

The tradition that esteems the human body as grace-filled in its sexual union also conflates miscarriage, the physical loss of a pregnancy, with murder in its rites. This dissonance elicits in me significant discomfiture. I see the balance of Orthodox tradition, as epitomized by the story of Anna and the *Joachim and Anna* icon, as offering an affirmative vision of humans as embodied beings, a vision that is a great beginning for a spiritual reflection on the physicality of conception as well as the ensuing aspects of motherhood. Yet I cannot ignore the disservice done by inaugurating and using the miscarriage rite for centuries.

I am not alone in my discomfiture. Orthodox people the world over are creatively encountering the need for a different way of approaching miscarriage. Pastoral guides are being written on this topic and new prayers for miscarriage are being blessed by a few bishops for use in their parishes. This is of vital importance in the Orthodox Church, which is a deeply liturgical tradition whose rites serve to nourish, uplift, and heal her people. A parish priest I know encourages women who miscarry to write a letter to the child, which he then tucks under the cloth on the altar, leaving it there for as long as she wants. This is one beautiful example of Christians working not just to handle their own discomfiture, but also to repair and strengthen their tradition.

For me, this points to one of the great challenges of being Orthodox Christian—or any type of Christian—or belonging to any ancient faith: those of us who choose to live within these traditions inevitably encounter their imperfect historical record. We can either ignore that imperfect historical record or we can work to make sense of it—and often it is *work* to make sense of it. This work within Orthodoxy involves, among other things, fashioning a new, respectful, and caring rite for the demise of a child in the womb, but the work at hand may look different in other traditions.

Setting aside the miscarriage rite, the fundamental appreciation for sexuality and procreation in Orthodoxy is seen in the ancient feast and icon of Anna and Joachim's conception of their daughter, Mary. This affirmation of the sexual experience and childbearing marks the genesis of the maternal body, and it grounds the exploration of other sources on the maternal body to come.

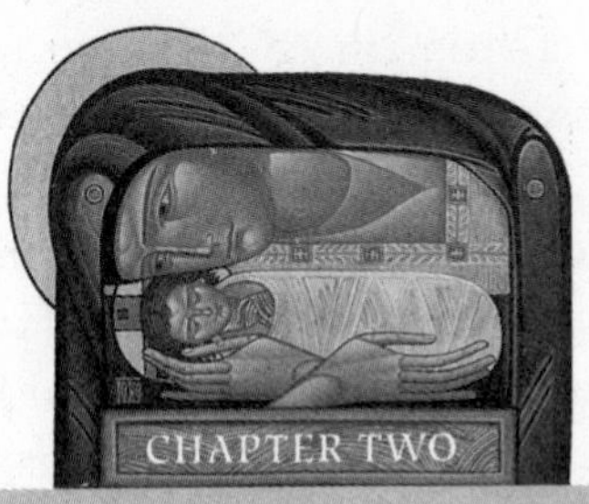

PREGNANCY

Soon after a new life is conceived, a woman experiences the changes that come with pregnancy: her breasts begin to swell as does her waist line, her blood supply increases, and a new and temporary organ, the placenta, is formed in her womb for the express purpose of nourishing her child in utero. Pregnancy also marks the beginning of the ascetical labor of motherhood; a woman's energy level is compromised, and her ability merely to rise swiftly from a chair is challenged—all for the sake of harboring new life. These challenges externally mark the beginning of the self-sacrifice that is integral to parenthood, to both mothers and fathers. A mother, however, gets an earlier start than a father on this opportunity for sacrifice, as her changing body makes demands on her even prior to birth.

Such demands were present during my pregnancies. The first two had their own physical challenges—pregnancy-induced carpal tunnel with my first and then sciatica with my second—in addition to the joys of hearing a heartbeat for the first time and feeling the flight of a small person inside of me.

Of course, nothing from those first two pregnancies compared to the intense experience of carrying triplets to thirty-six weeks.

In an effort to maximize the length of their gestation and increase the chances of high birth weights for the babies, both of which significantly improve the odds of healthy newborn multiples, I set out to gain a minimum of eighty-five pounds. This was especially daunting because I did not know I was carrying triplets until twelve weeks into the pregnancy, at which point I had gained no weight at all due to my relentless queasiness. As the pregnancy went on longer and longer—which pleased me because it gave the babies a better chance of being born healthy—my health problems multiplied, ultimately including severe edema, insomnia, gestational diabetes, and cholestasis (a liver problem presenting in its early stages as extreme itching from head to toe).

I was never officially put on bed rest, but I essentially experienced "couch rest" in the final months of the pregnancy; indeed, I was so big that it was hard to move. Throughout my pain and discomfort, I derived enormous comfort from knowing that the babies would be born stronger with each day that passed. In fact, it was the most satisfying suffering I have known. My experience is that much of this life's suffering is random and pointless and does not correlate with demonstrable, positive outcomes, but this was one case where pain really did mean gain. Literally. As I ballooned into some sort of preternatural parturient being, I also gained a deep reverence for my body that was supporting such dramatic change and sustaining four lives at once.

My Orthodox tradition shares a reverence for the pregnant form and for pregnancy in general. Scripture includes many references to being with child, including the repeated affirmation that God, as both fashioner and lover of all humans, intimately knows each person in the womb. This is the case in a passage from the Book of Psalms, which is chanted in a weekly rotation in Orthodox monasteries and is excerpted in lay services:

> For it was you who formed my inward parts;
> you knit me together in my mother's womb.
> I praise you, for I am fearfully and wonderfully made.
> Wonderful are your works;
> that I know very well.
> My frame was not hidden from you,
> when I was being made in secret,
> intricately woven in the depths of the earth.
> Your eyes beheld my unformed substance.
> In your book were written
> all the days that were formed for me,
> when none of them as yet existed.
> (Ps 139:13–16)

In addition to Scripture, Orthodox hymns repeatedly refer to the wonder of Mary's pregnancy with Christ. A hymn from fourth-century theologian-poet Ephrem the Syrian acknowledges the paradoxical mutuality of Christ's own embryonic state along with his role in the formation of others:

> While His body was being formed,
> His power was constructing all the members.
> While the fetus of the Son was being formed in the womb,
> He Himself was forming babes in the womb.[1]

The Akathist hymn to Mary (Akathist hymns being Orthodox service-length prayers dedicated to a particular saint), thought to date from the sixth century, likens Mary's womb to the baptismal font:

> Rejoice, you who illustrate the image of the font;
> Rejoice, you who wash away the stain of sin.
> Rejoice, water washing consciences clean;
> Rejoice, cup that mixes great joy.[2]

In its hymnic praise, the church acknowledges and celebrates the fact that Christ experienced Mary's womb in her pregnancy.

Pregnancy is also honored within the practices of the church. This happens organically, parish to parish. For example, the Orthodox liturgy contains several litanies that include prayers for everything from travelers to the local community, to those who are ill or held in captivity, and so on. Many of these are codified and found in most any printed copy of the Liturgy of Saint John Chrysostom (the eucharistic liturgy prayed most often), but local priests also have the liberty to insert particular petitions, and priests have been adding prayers for pregnant women to litanies in the eucharistic liturgy—sometimes by name—at least since the fourth century.[3]

Another example: when I was pregnant with the triplets and went up to the priest to be anointed during a service, I started to walk away after he made one sign of the cross in oil on my forehead, but he beckoned me back so that he could make three more. During certain services, a deacon or a priest "censes" the church, carrying an incense burner, sometimes with jingling bells attached, swinging it in front of each major icon of the church, blessing them, and often generally blessing the people in each side of the church. In some Russian parishes, the deacon or priest singles out pregnant women and censes them individually, while bowing.

In addition to these references to pregnancy in Scripture and song and these local practices, representations of pregnant saints are found in iconography, including depictions of Mary's pregnancy with Jesus Christ. By their very existence, these icons illustrate the esteem within Orthodoxy for the maternal body in its pregnant form. Furthermore, there are ways in which Mary's maternal body—especially in her pregnancy with Jesus Christ—was essential to the development and preservation of iconography in general.

That Christians would use the materials of the created world to fashion images of their savior and saints makes perfect sense—their God took on matter in order to appear in the world of his creation. There is a beauty in this thinking that constitutes a sort of "material piety" that supports both the creation of icons and the appreciation for the human body, and—particular to this book—the maternal body. As the expression attributed to eighth-century saint and defender of icons John of Damascus goes, "Show me the images that you venerate, and I will show you what you believe." In the case of the maternal body, the "what we believe" includes the entire Orthodox iconographic tradition, as well as specific icons that depict pregnant women. These are the themes of this chapter.

"What We Believe": Mary's Maternal Body in Icons

The existence of icons is predicated on the human body—the human body of Jesus Christ himself, and, therefore also the body of the one who gave him his humanity: his mother. In the incarnation, Jesus assumed a human body through Mary; the Divine entered thoroughly and completely into the material realm. In doing so, he sanctified the body. This embrace of the human form allows for images of Jesus Christ and the saints to be crafted and venerated in the Orthodox tradition. In turn, icons celebrate and safeguard the Christian theology of the body. Mary's maternal body played a particular role in both the development and preservation of icons.

Before exploring Mary's maternal body as relates to icons, I will offer a few words on iconography in general, especially for my readers who do not have images in their churches. For some, it comes as a shock to walk into an Orthodox church and see depictions of Jesus Christ, his mother, and the saints covering the walls and sometimes even the ceiling. I had a reverse sort of shock when I, as an eight-year-old, spent the night with a Methodist friend and went to her church in the morning; I was startled by what I perceived to be its sparseness, its austerity, with its blank white walls and the one, wooden cross in the apse.

The tradition of icons in the Orthodox Church is a part of an ancient continuum of Christian imagery, including frescos and mosaics from the second- and third-century catacombs of Rome, the burial grounds and holy places of early Christians. Predating even catacomb art, it is said that the Gospel writer Luke painted the first icon of Mary. It is easy to imagine that an image of her would be treated with affection, passed down through generations with loving care, copied, and displayed in holy places.

As the tradition of iconography developed, icons became stylized, showing elongated faces, special shadows placed around mouths, and so forth. This commonality of style is perhaps meant to emphasize the shared humanity of the saints and Jesus Christ. At the same time, icons are not generic; they do depict likenesses of actual people, as can be seen with recently canonized saints such as Saint Maria Skobtsova, for whom photos exist for comparison. It pleases me to consider that icons of Peter and Paul—which are of ancient provenance and always show Peter with white, curly hair, and Paul balding, with a dark beard—may well preserve their likenesses. Icons are not worshipped; they are venerated. Although they do have a didactic quality—details from a saint's life may be represented to tell the viewer of his or her life story—they are never exclusively instructive; they are also mystical, always leading the viewer toward the divine.

Once again, it is Jesus Christ's incarnation that is affirmed in Orthodox icons and that makes icons possible, but his mother is also critical for icons; because Mary is, at a minimum, functionally foundational to the incarnation, and she is also foundational to the icon. She gave Jesus his humanity, and thus there is a way in which her maternal body led to iconography. Furthermore, her presence was influential in understanding who Christ was and in the development of depictions of Christ in icons.

First, Mary's maternal body played a role in the doctrinal articulation of Christ's full humanity and full divinity. In the fifth century, the epithet of Theotokos for Mary—translated as "Mother of God" or "Birthgiver of God," which had been in devotional use at least since the late third century—was affirmed by the Council of Ephesus as validation of Christ's both fully human and fully divine natures, united in one person. The same council refuted other explanations of the relationship between Jesus Christ's humanity and divinity that rejected Mary as Theotokos and instead understood her as the mother of Jesus's human nature only (Christotokos). Mary was understood as having done the impossible: she gave God human form through her own flesh—her own maternal body.

This council-sanctioned recognition of Mary as Theotokos led to the fashioning of the well-known icon type of Mary closely holding Christ that is in common use to this day: the "She Who Points the Way" icon (Hodegetria). Mary and Christ are one visually unified form, which was a new development in the iconography of this period. They both look directly at the viewer, and one of Mary's hands, usually her right one, gestures to Christ; Mary is understood in these images as pointing the way to the Savior. Being held by his mother underscores his humanity, while her pointing to him indicates his divinity. Interestingly, Mary's role was viewed as so important to Christology that Christ is rarely depicted alone in this period of iconography.

"The Child in My Womb": Annunciation and Visitation

Over time, many ways of depicting Mary developed, including scenes of her Annunciation. One example that comes from twelfth-century Russia is a bit unusual, but germane to her pregnancy. In the more common Annunciation, the setting is Mary's home. Gabriel and Mary are seen together, with Mary often seated, sewing, or reading as Gabriel approaches her with respect. Such depictions of this encounter have an ancient history, going back to at least the fourth century.

Pregnancy

The variation of the Annunciation icon under discussion here is the *Ustyug Annunciation* icon from twelfth-century Russia, with a prototype likely dating to the ninth century (see Figure 2). It was probably produced in the region of Novgorod, but it is called "Ustyug" because of its association with the village of Ustyug in local histories and saints' hagiographies. The *Ustyug Annunciation* is of historical note because it is one of the few icons to have survived the Mongol invasion of Russia in the thirteenth century. In this icon, the angel Gabriel is seen on the viewer's left, with his heels not quite touching the ground, which suggests the dynamism of the event of the Annunciation. Mary herself looks at the viewer, while holding a distaff wound with thread in preparation for weaving a curtain for the Temple—the work that she is traditionally depicted as engaged in when Gabriel encounters her. While it lacks many of the other usual homey details of Annunciation icons, the *Ustyug Annunciation* includes a noteworthy addition: a visible, shadowy Christ in Mary's womb.

In Mary's translucent midsection hovers an image of a childlike Jesus Christ. Even though it is the moment of his conception, he is depicted as a fully formed baby. This creative license is purposeful, to show that he has, through his mother's form, taken on a demonstrably human body. He wears just a loincloth, as he will on his last day. His hand is extended in a traditional blessing, both of his mother and of the viewer. At the top of the icon sits a tiny half-mandorla—a decorative ellipsis that is a common motif in iconography—that encloses an adult Jesus Christ also in a blessing posture. Here is evidence of the work of the church councils in articulating Christology: Mary is taking Jesus Christ, her savior and king, into her own body, giving him flesh and harboring him there until the time for his birth.

The comparative sparseness of this depiction of the Annunciation emphasizes Mary's pregnant form. In this way, the *Ustyug Annunciation* beautifully testifies to the enduring appeal and importance of understanding Mary's maternal body as sacred—an understanding generated by Christ's sanctification of pregnancy by his experience in his own mother's womb and, therefore, an understanding that is rightfully extended to all maternal bodies.

The pregnant form is also represented in the *Visitation* icon. This icon engages the story from the first chapter of the Gospel of Luke, of pregnant Mary visiting her cousin Elizabeth, who is herself pregnant with John the Baptist. The Feast of the Visitation has an unusual liturgical history. While long honored in imagery, it was only added to the Orthodox calendar (March 30) relatively recently: in the late nineteenth century, a monk who took care of a church built on the site of the Visitation near Jerusalem successfully urged the Orthodox Church to include it. The Feast of the Visitation has been celebrated for much longer in the Christian West, where it was declared a universal feast (July 2) by Pope Urban VI in the fourteenth century and was celebrated by the Franciscans even earlier than that. However, given that the Annunciation is March 25 and the Nativity of John the Baptist is June 24, celebrating the Visitation—which clearly takes place between the two events, according to Scripture—on July 2 made no chronological sense. Therefore, the calendric reforms of Vatican II included an adjustment, and now, with few exceptions (notably Germany and Slovakia), the Visitation is celebrated on May 31. Images of the Visitation predate the official inclusion of this feast on both calendars; indeed, they date back at least to the fifth century, as found on small oil vessels used by pilgrims.

In Luke, the Visitation is described as follows:

> In those days Mary set out and went with haste to a Judean town in the hill country, where she entered the house of Zechariah and greeted Elizabeth. When Elizabeth heard Mary's greeting, the child leaped in her womb. And Elizabeth was filled with the Holy Spirit and exclaimed with a loud cry, "Blessed are you among women, and blessed is the fruit of your womb. And why has this happened to me, that the mother of my Lord comes to me? For as soon as I heard the sound of your greeting, the child in my womb leaped for joy. And blessed is she who believed that there would be a fulfillment of what was spoken to her by the Lord." (Luke 1:39–45)

Like the *Ustyug Annunciation*, some Visitation icons include visibly pregnant mothers with shadowy images of a child in the womb. More commonly, Visitation icons simply show the expectant cousins greeting each other in a loving embrace. This is an intimate portrait of this moment between these two women; they are usually shown cheek to cheek as in the contemporary Russian *Visitation*, created by female iconographer Olga Shalamova (see Figure 3). In this icon, the background and frame are delicately patterned in a fresh manner, yet all the elements of Mary and Elizabeth themselves are entirely consistent with the details of ancient versions of the Visitation icon.

Elizabeth's garments flutter behind her, showing that the two women have rushed into each other's arms in a way that is reminiscent of the urgency only otherwise seen in the icon of Anna and Joachim; Luke does note that Mary went to Elizabeth "with haste." The robes of the two women are voluminous such that their pregnancies are not obvious to the viewer (though, technically, only Elizabeth would have been showing at this point in her pregnancy). This is reflective of women's clothing in the ancient world where expectant mothers loosened their robes to accommodate abdominal expansion and did not trade them in for figure-hugging maternity clothes. In this icon, Mary reaches her left hand toward Elizabeth's abdomen, perhaps acknowledging her expectant state. Their embrace is intimate, and this is another way in which this icon is reminiscent of the *Joachim and Anna* icon—these are the only two icons of which I know that include two adults embracing (I qualify "adults" because there are scores of icons of Mary and Jesus Christ in an embrace). This physical intimacy suggests to me that Mary and Elizabeth feel a kinship beyond their blood kinship as cousins; they also feel a kinship through their shared experience of motherhood. All these elements of the *Visitation* icon make for an image that honors their maternal bodies.

The story of the Visitation also speaks to the divine connection possible through the maternal body. When Mary sees her cousin Elizabeth, she calls to Elizabeth. John—through his mother—hears in Mary's voice the good news that his savior is being carried in Mary's womb. He recognizes this from inside of his mother and jumps gladly in response. Elizabeth knows that John moves in response to Mary's greeting: "As soon as I heard the sound of your greeting, the child in my womb leaped for joy" (Luke 1:44). It is through the two mothers' bodies that John gains access to the knowledge that Jesus Christ is near. This narrative provides a nuanced

Figure 1. *Joachim and Anna*. See page 10

Figure 2. *Ustyug Annunciation*. See page 29

Figure 3.
Visitation.
See page 31

Figure 4.
Nativity.
See page 42

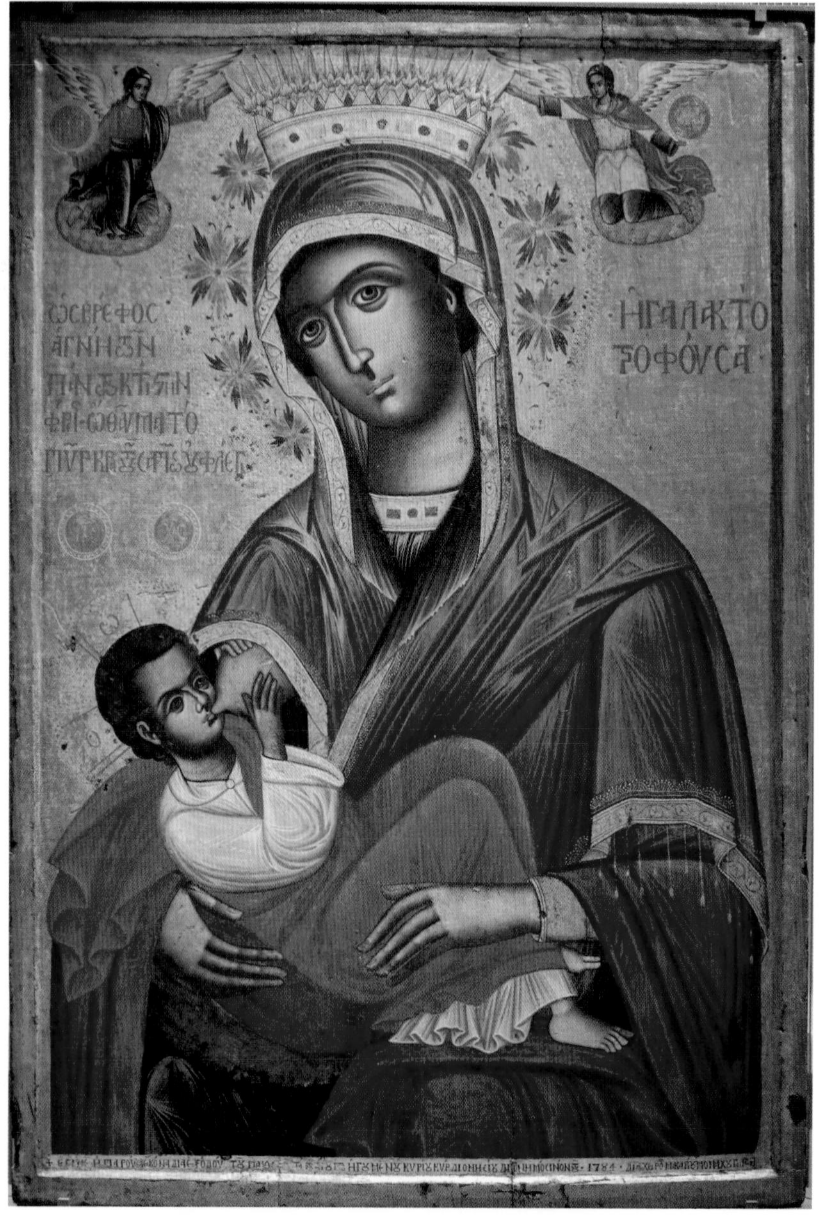

Figure 5. *Milk Giver (Galaktotrophousa)*. See page 70

portrait of the maternal body at work and suggests that knowledge of Jesus Christ can be acquired by and through it.

Maternal Images

In the pregnant maternal body, a mother cannot escape her embodied, incarnate nature. At some other times in life, one may be capable of living as though the brain is the only organ that matters, but this approach is not possible during pregnancy. Pregnancy *is* physicality. Even nontriplet, medically uncomplicated pregnancies are physically intense. The sheer effort of carrying around extra pounds that squirm is enough to remind the mother of the constant presence of her full body; she is continuously brought back into her physical being. The unique intimacy with another body inside of her also creates a new consciousness of her own embodied reality. This physicality does not relent after the birth—an extremely physical act in itself. Nor does it relent during the postpartum healing of the mother's body; nor during her days, months, or years of lactation; nor indeed anytime soon, given her physical care of and her proximity to her child, which is experienced by all mothers, whether they are biological or adoptive. It is thus very fitting that the Orthodox Church would acknowledge and celebrate the maternal body in the development of the defense of iconography and honor it in specific icons.

In particular, the two icons examined here that depict pregnancy—the *Ustyug Annunciation* and the *Visitation*—display and honor the maternal body. Beyond these two specific icon types, few occasions exist for the depiction of pregnant women in icons. Festal commemorations of motherhood and childbearing tend to address three moments: conception, birth, and presentation in the temple—not, say, mid-pregnancy, when a woman is rotund with new life. The two icons examined here—though theologically sound—represent the less common manner of depicting their events.

Yet, change is underway in current depictions of the maternal body in icons. Visitation icons that show visible babes in the womb are becoming more common. The appearance of one such icon in the chapel of a conventional women's monastery in California suggests that this icon has entered the mainstream.[4] Icons of a Yup'ick midwife, Olga Michael of Kwethluk, Alaska, who is on the way to sainthood, show her ministering to expectant mothers—an icon composition that has no precedent. Certain depictions of Mary in the Nativity of Jesus Christ icons are becoming more common, as I will discuss in the next chapter. The strongest reason for these changes may be that there are now a significant number of women studying and creating Orthodox icons.

Iconography is not an innovative tradition; it does not place a premium on novelty or welcome a lot of change. However, it is—and it must be—a *creative* tradition that is spirit-driven. Women are now, for the first time, bringing a female eye and hand to icons. This may mean that new, legitimate icon types are inspired or that icon types with an established tradition, such as the Visitation, are popularized. I hope for an efflorescence of Orthodox iconography in which female iconographers work on all iconographic subjects and especially bring their experiences of women's and mothers' bodies to their work, including sacred images of the maternal body.

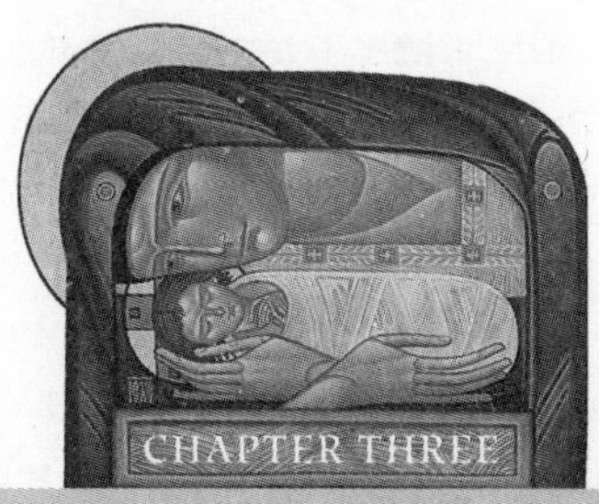

BIRTHGIVING

A typical pregnancy comes to an end after about forty weeks, but that end is, in fact, a tremendous beginning. A woman's water may break, or her uterus may simply begin to contract, first erratically and then rhythmically. The baby moves into position, typically head down, and is pushed through the vaginal canal by the contracting uterus and the mother's focused efforts. The tip-top of the baby's head, the "crown," is seen first. Finally, the newborn issues forth from the mother's womb, emerging wet and possibly blood- or stool-streaked, into air and light and cold. The umbilical cord, the strand that physically connected mother and child through the pregnancy, is cut. Then comes the delivery of the afterbirth, the precious organ of the placenta that nourished the child within. The parents embrace the baby, who is wrapped up and held close to stay warm. The mother, in whose body this baby was conceived, whose frame was laden with this new life for nine months, is finally able to hold, see, and touch her child.

My own childbirth experiences were not typical. With my firstborn, I experienced a Caesarean section about forty hours after my water started to leak, after many hours of hard labor, and after my cervix had become too swollen for delivery. I asked my obstetrician what would have happened had I given birth unattended, say, in the wilderness a hundred years ago. His answer was frank: "One or both of you would have died." I was newly appreciative of living when and where I did. My second child was born by way of a scheduled C-section recommended by what in retrospect was probably an overly cautious doctor, and the triplets were also delivered by C-section, as is the standard of care in the United States in triplet pregnancies.

Several people have made comments to me along the lines of, "Well, since you didn't have a *vaginal* birth, you didn't really *give birth*." These remarks used to sting because, as I would suppose is the case with many women who have C-sections, I feel that I did miss out; I wanted to experience a vaginal delivery. After further reflection, however, it became clear to me I did *give birth*; that my body and my own agency were very much a part of bringing each one of my children forth from the womb. Furthermore, and I believe this got to the core of these cutting comments, my C-section status in no way diminishes my authenticity as a mother.

I wish to underscore and extend this point to note that the same is true for the adoptive mother who arrives at the hospital to receive her son from his biological mother, or the adoptive mother who, say, arrives in Korea to receive her five-year old daughter from an agency. All of these women are to be equally understood and celebrated as mothers. Whatever physical part of the biological process any particular mother did not experience does not disqualify her from authentic motherhood.

As for my own embodied experience of birthgiving, the most exceptional moment in the process came when I first looked into each baby's eyes. Each time, I was reminded of a description I once read of a kayaker's encounter with a whale. The whale surfaced slowly and purposefully right next to the kayak and tilted its large form in order to behold the kayaker with one mysterious eye. When I first held gaze with one of my babies, I, too, experienced the sacramental quality of communing with a being at once mysterious, novel, and perfect. Most memorable among those encounters with my children is when I saw my first daughter. While I was strapped into my own sort of kayak—the C-section table—and awake throughout the C-section thanks to today's anesthesiology, my husband brought her over to me. I looked into her looming eyes and noticed a beautiful aberration: swimming in the gray-blue birth color of her right iris was a dark pool of brown. This mark—an aberration in pigment called a "sectoral heterochromia"—remains with her today, and to me it symbolizes her sheer uniqueness and beauty among creatures. I will never forget those first moments of shared gaze with her or with my other children.

My understanding of my birthgiving experiences is also informed by the sources of my Orthodox tradition. Before I was wheeled in for the C-section with my firstborn, I placed, on the pillow next to my head, an icon of Saint Anna, my own saint, shown giving birth to her daughter Mary (the Nativity of the Mother of God icon), such was the connection I felt between my own birthgiving and that of the women in my tradition. It was quite a conversation piece in the operating room.

That icon is just one example of the fact that birth, perhaps even more than conception or pregnancy, is a focal point in Orthodoxy. This is quite literally true: the Orthodox year begins with a birth—the first major feast of the church year is the Nativity of the Mother of God on September 9. (Interestingly, the Catholic liturgical year also revolves around a birth, starting with Advent in preparation of the birth of Jesus Christ.) The words lauding the auspicious birth of Jesus Christ resound in our ears in every liturgy, every Vespers, every prayer of the Hours. Images of birthgiving are present in any Orthodox church: the Feasts of the Nativity of Mary and the Nativity of Jesus Christ will often be along the top of the icon screen in front of the altar.

One of the greatest testaments to the reverence with which the church treats birth is the fact that one of the very earliest established Marian feasts is for the express purpose of celebrating Mary's birthgiving. Today this feast is called the "Synaxis of the Theotokos" on the Orthodox calendar and has been celebrated the day after Christmas since before the fifth century. Twentieth-century theologian Father Alexander Schmemann reflects on the significance of this feast: "[Jesus Christ's] humanity—concretely and historically—is the humanity He received from Mary. His body is, first of all, her body. His life is her life. This feast, the assembly in honor of the Theotokos, is probably the most ancient feast of Mary in the Christian tradition."[1] It is this birthgiving—Mary's labor and delivery of Christ—that is the focus of this chapter.

"Beyond Human Understanding": Mary Gave Birth to God

I choose Mary's story not without pause. When I explained to an acquaintance about my initial search for theological sources on motherhood, she said, "Well, you are going to have to look for sources other than the Virgin Mary." When, puzzled by this statement, I asked her why she thought Mary was out of bounds for a consideration of motherhood, she told me that she sees Mary as so elevated, so exceptional that she has nothing to offer normal mothers. This person is Catholic, but Orthodox Christians also sometimes elevate Mary beyond reproach in such a way that she is also beyond *approach*. Whether this is appropriate or not is, I believe, an open question, especially when it comes to her birthgiving.

The Orthodox tradition expresses its understanding of Mary's birthgiving in different ways over time and space. Whereas Catholics articulate a clear, doctrinal understanding of her virginity before, during, and after childbirth (meaning both abstention from sexual intercourse and the denial of any change to her physical body during childbirth) and engage with the minutiae of her virginal state during childbirth in fine detail, we Orthodox have no dogmatic position on the matter of her physical state during childbirth. Orthodoxy does dedicate some thought to her virginity during childbirth—mostly in the context of Old Testament typologies and prophesies—and some of that thought indicates that the church is of a mixed mind on this subject.

On the one hand, Mary's title of Theotokos or "Birthgiver of God" includes, as noted by Mariologist Mary B. Cunningham, "the whole process of conception and child-bearing: it is thus impossible, according to this tradition, to distinguish separate phases in this process."[2] In this way, Mary's entire biological process of becoming a mother is understood as exceptional—she was the *Mother of God*. On the other hand, the church in texts, doctrine, icons, hymns, and homilies affirms Mary's fully human experience of motherhood after her exceptional conception at the Annunciation—she was God's *human mother*.

The particulars of Mary's birthgiving are neither enshrined in Scripture nor solidified in Orthodox doctrine; they are theological details of her life that have been perceived in different ways as the church's perception of her shifts throughout time and place, and this is especially reflected in the church's hymnography. One example comes from a service for the Nativity of Christ. Because this material is concerned with exaltation of the wonderful and exceptional birth of Jesus Christ, it may be no surprise to find reference to the Birthgiver's pain-free birth:

> Coming forth in the flesh,
> O Word coeternal with the Father,
> from a Mother who suffered no pangs of birth....[3]

However, Saint Ephrem's hymnic portrayal of Mary's experience of giving birth to Jesus Christ rings a little differently. Ephrem creatively explores Mary's authentic, painful birthgiving experience:

> The First-born entered the womb, but the pure
> one perceived Him not.
> He arose and emerged with birth-pangs, and the
> fair one felt Him.
> Glorious and hidden His entry, despised and
> visible His emergence,
> Since He is God at his entry, but human at His
> emergence.[4]

In just two examples from the hymnographic tradition to the Orthodox Church, a range of views of the experience of Mary's birthgiving of her son is expressed. The fact that *in partu*, the descriptive term used to refer to her virginity during childbirth, is a Latin term, a Western Christian term, and that there is no equivalent Orthodox Christian term, says a lot about my tradition's attention to this issue. Perhaps the bottom line here is best reflected in Mary Cunningham's observation that, ultimately, the liturgical tradition "assumes that the mystery of Mary's birth-giving and Christ's incarnation remain beyond human understanding."[5]

It is worth noting that all the theological thinking on Mary's experience during childbirth thus far was done by men, not by women, much less by people who have actually experienced childbirth—mothers. This is another theological area in which I eagerly look to female contributions over time. My sympathies as a constructive theologian chafe at single-minded expressions of Mary's birth as supernatural in character, for christological reasons (his humanity is dependent on her humanity) and mariological reasons (she is human, not a goddess), and I understand her experience as akin and accessible to us mundane mothers. This is why I chose to refer to her with her given name, "Mary," rather than use one of her honorifics, like Mother of God or Theotokos, as is often done in Orthodox writing; I wish to remind myself and my readers that—although the most perfect human—she is still a human person like the rest of us. In fact, I think it is critical for the church's understanding of her and the incarnation that she be remembered in this way. Moreover though, I wish to preserve the creative freedom that allows theologians and hymnographers of the church to hold variant understandings of Mary's birthgiving.

I must save a theological treatise on this topic for another day because I wish instead to turn to another aspect of Mary's birthgiving, one that is also very much related to her embodied and human experience of labor and delivery: her time of contemplation just after giving birth to Jesus Christ. Luke tells of this moment of contemplation, and it is witnessed in the iconographic tradition of the church for at least sixteen hundred years in the Nativity of Christ icon. It is this contemplative moment that Mary experiences in her maternal body that is exemplary for mothers today.

"Full of Deep Meaning": The Posture of Mary

The icon for the Feast of the Nativity of Jesus Christ featured here was composed for a monastery in Saint Petersburg by a pair of contemporary Russian iconographers, Philip Davydov and Olga Shalamova (see Figure 4). The composition and details are much the same as ancient prototypes of this icon, including those seen on fifth-century pilgrims' holy oil jars as well as many Nativity icons today. The viewer is offered a glimpse of the scene just after Christ's birth, including the people, animals, and things included in the combined gospel birth narratives: the magi, the shepherds, the angels, the swaddling clothes, the manger, and so on.

Two other elements, the ox and the ass, are positioned closer to Jesus Christ than any human or angel and seem to be affectionately reaching to nuzzle him. Their presence is not directly mentioned in the Gospels (although we do know that Jesus was born in a place where animals slept), but in the Book of Isaiah: "The ox knows its owner, and the donkey its master's crib" (Isa 1:3). The presence of these two humble creatures warms my animal-loving heart and affirms a basic tenet of the Feast of the Nativity—that all of creation rejoices at the birth of Jesus Christ.

Joseph, Mary's betrothed, is also present, and he is seen here in the lower right-hand corner of the icon. Not seen here, but in other versions of this icon, there is an old, bent-over, bearded man next to Joseph, who is understood to represent the devil, or at least temptation made manifest. Although neither the Gospels nor the *Book of James* mentions this character, both sources allude to Joseph's struggle to accept the pregnancy of his betrothed (e.g., Matt 1:18–21). Over time, this aspect of the narrative was given visual representation in the form of Joseph's companion. It is interesting to note that in many contemporary versions of this icon, Joseph is still sitting off to the side, looking a little adrift and forlorn, but the devil-figure is dropped from the cast of characters.

It is also hard to know what to make of the two women in the lower left corner who appear to be bathing Jesus. These women come not from Scripture but from the *Book of James*, and contrary to the meaning attributed to Mary's reclined posture, they testify to a supernatural birthgiving, as one of them is reported to literally insert her finger inside of Mary to determine if she is a physically intact virgin,[6] and—in another sense—they testify to a human birthgiving experience because one of them is reported to be a midwife, pointing to the need for aid during Mary's labor and a quite human birthgiving.

Most central to this image, and most germane to our consideration, is the figure of Mary. The viewer's gaze goes directly to her. She is central, disproportionately large, and positioned on a bright red blanket, a sort of bedroll for travelers in the ancient world. Even though the Feast of the

Nativity is focused on the birth of God, Mary is the visual focus of this icon. This is no accident.

Her centrality here underscores that the incarnation is about the rebirth of all of creation, an act that is fittingly accomplished through motherhood. As a *mother*, Mary is the agent for a cosmic rebirth. Nothing escapes these sanctifying waters of childbirth that flooded in a cave, in the darkness, two thousand years ago. Of course, at the time of Christ's birth, the crucifixion and the resurrection have yet to come; therefore, the work is not yet fully accomplished. But Orthodoxy understands the incarnation as an event suffused with grace and brimming with hope. Thus, her centrality in Nativity icons is both intentional and appropriate.

Also meaningful are Mary's posture and gaze. Regarding her posture: she is reclined, leaning back on her left elbow. This is typical for Nativity icons, and it is often explained as showing that she has just experienced the physical exertion of childbirth; she is tired and now she is resting after labor. As twentieth-century iconographer and art historian Leonid Ouspensky writes, "In the great majority of images of Christ's Nativity the Mother of God is lying down, showing in her posture a great lassitude. Which should remind those of us who pray of the undoubtedly human nature of the Babe."[7]

There is another variation of the Nativity of Christ icon type in which, instead of reclining in postpartum repose, Mary is sitting upright, in a position of adoration or veneration of her son. Sometimes this variation is mistakenly (and usually pejoratively) attributed to "Western Christian influence," suggesting it was not something that appeared in the Christian East until it was introduced through the Christian West at a relatively late date, usually named as the Renaissance. This is simply not the case. There are ancient examples from the Christian East of Mary in more upright postures from at least the late first millennium, although it may well be true that there was an increase in this representation in the post-Renaissance era. In these more upright versions, Mary appears to be unperturbed by childbirth, unaffected by the experience of labor and delivery; this seems to reflect the thinking, as noted earlier, that her childbirth experience was every bit as exceptional and supernatural as was her conception of Jesus Christ.

The coexistence of these icon variants in the Christian East, each with its own statement about Mary's birthgiving experience, illustrates the theological flexibility in the Orthodox ways of encountering Mary and her birthgiving of Jesus Christ. Ouspensky affirms this flexibility and defends these dichotomous ways of depicting Mary, saying that "the posture of the Mother of God is always full of deep meaning and connected with dogmatic problems, which arose at different times or places. Alterations of this posture emphasize, according to need, either the Divine or the human nature of the Savior."[8] It seems that iconography, even with its loyal adherence to tradition, allows for a more fluid, more responsive, and more interactive relationship with time and place than theological treatises typically afford.

Pondering in Her Heart

Turning back to the *Nativity* icon, Mary's gaze is meaningful. Here in the Davydov-Shalamova *Nativity*, as well as in nearly all Nativity icons in which Mary is reclined, she looks not at her son, but away from him, in contrast to the upright version, in which she is usually shown looking directly at him. This is strange—would not most mothers be engrossed in their newborns? I was certainly smitten with beholding my new babies, as I related at the beginning of the chapter. Some imagery in icons has a clear theological or scriptural point of origin such as the presence of the magi, but, in other cases, the original theological significance of a detail—if there was one—is not clear, and this invites theological speculation, especially since icons are living images that continue to speak to the faithful, offering different inspiration in different times and places. So, why Mary looks away from her son in the "reclined" version of the icon is a subject of theological debate for those who study icons. Some suggest that she turns away from her son in order to welcome everyone to him, but her gaze does not seem to be particularly welcoming. Others propose that her gaze has a prophetic quality, envisioning what is to come with her son's end on the cross. Yet Mary has yet to hear the words of Simeon, who will tell her to expect a piercing of her own soul (Luke 2:34–35).

Just as the rest of the image is full of details from Scripture, I choose to interpret Mary's gaze as also scriptural. I believe it shows us the moment after giving birth in which Luke tells us that "Mary treasured all these words and pondered them in her heart" (Luke 2:19). As angels sing and magi travel and shepherds visit, she dedicates a bit of time to contemplating who Christ is, her relationship to him, what she has experienced, and all of the mystery around her. Of course, she could well ponder such matters while gazing *at* her son, but by showing her looking away from Christ, and gazing calmly into the distance, this version of the Nativity icon suggests to me that she is actively engaged in such contemplation.

In this way, Mary can be understood as the first Christian contemplative. A few centuries will pass before the terminology develops and practices are passed down from spiritual fathers and mothers to spiritual sons and daughters, but it is not a stretch to see her as a protopractitioner of "Prayer of the Heart." In this Orthodox prayer tradition, the heart is understood, for one thing, as the place in which the mind and the body unite, and is the place in which we are best able to connect with the Divine. Dedication to the practice of particular types of contemplative prayer such as Prayer of the Heart promotes this connection.

Conceived of this way, contemplative prayer neither denies the body nor intellectualizes the project of prayer; instead it creates an authentic space in which a person is able to be present with an awareness of both oneself and of God. Metropolitan Kallistos Ware speaks to this when he writes that the heart "signifies not merely the emotions and affections, but the moral and spiritual center of the total human person, the ground and focal point of our created being, the deep self."[9] Mary, immediately after her birthgiving experience, is capable of an awareness of her "deep self," which then allows her to have an awareness of God, not only because she has direct experience with him, but also because she dedicates the time to cultivate that awareness through contemplation. She quiets her mind, sinks into her body, and finds her connection with God there—right after giving birth.

In her choice to ponder all these things in her heart, Mary provides a model for mothers to emulate. Of all the offices in life, raising children is one of the most physically, emotionally, and spiritually intense, and, like Mary, a mother needs to pause and ponder who she is and her relationship to her children and to God. In our own time, the competing claims on our attention as mothers are legion, and it takes an act of will to set them aside and create such a space for pondering. There is no more inspiring example than Mary, of all people, taking the time to ponder these things in her heart. If this is something she, most sublime of all humans, needed to do, then surely we also need this. If this is something she could make time for, of all times just after having given birth to Jesus, then surely we have time for this. Through her example, we are invited to create our own maternal contemplation.

Embodied Contemplative

I began this chapter musing about my tradition's mixed encounter with Mary's body during her birthgiving experience, and I wish to extend these reflections here at the end, to how my tradition has understood virginity and the body over time. This is important because these things have colored how we view the maternal body, and this bears on how we are able to see Mary as an embodied maternal contemplative, as in the *Nativity* icon.

Various theologians of the early church became deeply invested in Mary's virginity because it served as a pillar of their defense of virginity as the superior mode of Christian life. As one consequence of this line of thinking, consecrated virginity was valorized at the expense of family life, including motherhood, which led to a negative view of the human body and sexuality, including the maternal body. As church historian Jaroslav Pelikan writes, "Christian asceticism expressed itself in a rejection of the body that appeared to deny that God has created it, and therefore in a revulsion at sexuality that equated it with immorality."[10] The theologians who thus defined Christian asceticism were male; these systems of thought about the human body and spirit were composed by men.

It is important to note that not all Christian versions of asceticism or monasticism include such dualistic visions of the body, but, even so, these dualistic visions were quite influential over the centuries and they have negatively influenced our perception of Mary. This was lamented by Orthodox theologian Elisabeth Behr-Sigel: "In the atmosphere of a monastic spirituality in which ascetical motivations predominate, in which sex, and especially woman, was often seen as synonymous with sin, the piety surrounding Mary has not always escaped the temptation of 'angelism.' In relation to Mary, this 'angelism' seems to be a real heresy....The result is that the Mother of God is radically separated from ordinary women who can neither recognize themselves in her nor be recognized in her."[11] It is this separation that prompted my acquaintance to express skepticism about the applicability of Mary for my work on the maternal body.

Fortunately, this is not the only understanding of Mary in the church, and, indeed, there is flexibility within Orthodox thought and imagery of Mary that allows for engaging with her motherhood and her birthgiving experience in different ways. I am curious to see how her birthgiving will be portrayed and expressed as more and more women who have actually experienced birthgiving become theologians and iconographers.

The dominant image of the reclined, resting Mary in the Nativity icons is an image that works against any lingering angelism of Mary, against any negative view of the maternal body. Here is a woman who has just experienced childbirth, whose body is fatigued, whose mind is probably overwhelmed, and who has gone to her heart as the place in which to ponder all these things. *Mary is an embodied contemplative.* She is an embodied contemplative immediately in the wake of birthgiving. She experiences her pondering as a postpartum mother; resting in that space of physical enervation, she contemplates. This is not angelism; this is not disembodied contemplation; this is not dualistic prayer that privileges the mind and denigrates the body. Instead, this is a woman, who, after one of the most supremely physical human acts, in the midst of the hubbub of visitors and gifts, and heavenly host singing and so on, turns silent, and heeds the words of the psalmist: "Be still, and know that I am God!" (Ps 46:10). In so doing, Our Mother of Stillness provides an imitable and inspiring example of embodied maternal contemplation.

POSTPARTUM

The first few postpartum months are intensely physical as the mother recovers from childbirth and adjusts to her new maternal body. After growing accustomed to her pregnant form just in time to give birth, now everything changes. She experiences lochia (postpartum bleeding), breasts swelling with milk, and an abdomen that does not instantly (or ever) return to its original shape, no matter what happens in the movies.

The new mother is not alone as she adjusts to her altered body; she has a newborn. The care for her baby is also intensely physical, and intimately so. A mother spends hours each day holding, feeding, bathing, wiping, caressing, burping, changing, and soothing her newborn, hopefully with help from her husband, family, and friends. She likely does all of this on little sleep and addled by the intensity of the situation. An early phase occurs in adoptive motherhood as well; even though the journey and the timing are different, the task of physically caring for one's child for the first time is also intense, and no less significant. An adoptive mother's physical self is marked by her motherhood as well, be it the callouses a friend developed from brushing her three daughters' very thick hair, or the fine spray of laughter lines around the eyes of another mother.

I am physically altered by motherhood in many ways, but especially by all three of my pregnancies. After the birth of my firstborn, my hair changed color from strawberry blonde to a much darker red in the span of a few days, a bizarre occurrence on which everyone at the hospital remarked but no one could explain. My second pregnancy left a calling card of silky stretch marks. What is most memorable from any postpartum time, though, is the relentless physical labor my maternal body experienced in caring for newborn triplets. I would change the diapers of all three, nurse each one (carefully noting on a chart who nursed first, to remember to nurse that baby last next time), then they would need their diapers changed again, then it would be time to nurse them again, and on and on. I recall that time as one of the most physically intense eras of my life—I went to bed spent each night, like a farmer during harvest season.

In addition to the adjustments to all the changes in my body and the work of caring for these new little people, I experienced my own Orthodox tradition's rite of passage for the postpartum time of motherhood. Around six weeks after their birth, my husband and I packed the triplets and the big kids into our (newly purchased-to-accommodate-seven) van and drove to church where the triplets and I experienced our "churching." The churching rite is celebrated when a mother comes back to church after childbirth. In it, the newborn is warmly welcomed into the church for the first time: "And bless the child which has been born of her. Increase him [her]; sanctify him [her]; enlighten him [her]; render him [her] chaste; and endow him [her] with good understanding. For Thou hast brought him [her] into being, and hast shown him [her] the physical light, and hast appointed him [her] in due time to be counted worthy of spiritual light."[1] As referenced in the anticipation of "spiritual light," the baby is not baptized at this time, but will be baptized soon—sometimes the same day, other times weeks or a couple of months later.

For me, each churching marked a point of transition between the intensity of the early weeks of motherhood to a less acute, though perhaps no less arduous, era of established motherhood. I believe this is part of the good of this rite. In the ancient world, women were more or less cloistered in their homes after childbirth, and their churching was not just a return to liturgical services, but also a return to normal activities. Even today, women tend to lay low after childbirth, and obstetricians and midwives often suggest six or so weeks of rest. It seems appropriately sequenced first to resume church attendance before, say, heading to the grocery store or returning to the office. It is lovely that this return to one's everyday routine is sanctified in the church, with prayers for the well-being of mother and baby.

Yet churching fell almost entirely into disuse in the Christian West and, though still widely used, it is being sharply questioned in the Christian East because it was actually not created with the intention of marking a woman's emergence after childbirth, even though it functions that way. It is under suspicion because it includes an alleged connection between childbirth and "uncleanness" or "impurity" that is both harsh on the ear and theologically unsound. For example, the first prayer includes these lines: "Purify her [the mother], therefore, from every sin and from every defilement [often translated as "filth"] as she now draws near to Thy holy church; and let her be counted worthy to partake, uncondemned, of Thy Holy Mysteries."[2]

This is the biggest breach in the Orthodox Church between theology and practice pertaining to motherhood. In contrast to the celebration of the maternal form in other Orthodox sources, like the *Ustyug Annunciation* icon as seen in chapter 2, here a disassociation is made between a mother's body and the goodness of its life-creating work. Though the history of the theological concept of *impurity* is complex (and will be explored below), *impurity* is nearly always equated with *sin* in Christian usage. Therefore, the churching rite frames a woman's experience of motherhood with the sentiment that the childbearing process renders her sinful, and the same message is communicated to her husband, the rest of her family, and everyone in the community. This is a grievous state of affairs.

Even so, I believe that churching holds great possibility for a ritual of hospitality shown to a mother and her baby. The churching rite in the Christian East and West—its history, its flaws, and its possibility—will be the theme of this chapter, with a special eye to seeing how churching might be best reconciled with the church's theology of the body, and therefore, appropriately honor the maternal body.

"Wash Away Her Bodily and Spiritual Uncleanness"

Found in the Orthodox Christian compendium of prayers for a parish priest known as *The Great Book of Needs*, churching, formally known as the "Prayer for a Woman on the Fortieth Day of Childbirth," takes place at church, in the presence of the whole community. It essentially consists of three prayers for the health and salvation of the newborn and two prayers for the well-being of the mother—and for her "purity."

As noted earlier, the very first prayer in the Orthodox churching rite intimates that the experience of childbirth leaves the mother in need of purification from both "sin" and "every defilement," and that she is therefore unworthy of communion in her postpartum state. The same emphasis is present in the second prayer for the mother when the priest asks, "O Lord our God, Who didst come for the salvation of the human race, come also upon Thy servant, *Name*, and count her worthy, through the prayers of Thine honorable Priest, of entrance into the temple of Thy Glory. Wash away her bodily and spiritual uncleanness, in the completion of the forty days. Make her worthy also of the communion of Thy precious Body and Blood."[3] The prayers are clear: this is not an abstract or strictly spiritual impurity, it is *bodily*—the very maternal body is understood to be unclean.

The ancient versions of churching in the West were even more concerned with the impurity of the mother than the Christian East, so it is not hard to see why churching is, with rare exceptions, not practiced at all today in the West. After Vatican II, the Catholic Church essentially condensed churching into one prayer for the mother without any reference to impurity and inserted it into the baby's baptismal service. Though it did not have staying power in much of the Protestant world, a churching rite was retained in the early days of the Protestant Reformation, and Martin Luther himself admirably worked to transform the rite from one of purification to one of thanksgiving, convinced that there is nothing impure about childbirth. Protestant forms of churching faded over time, though, except for within the Anglican Communion, where it was practiced well into the twentieth century, but now is largely out of use.

In a tradition guided by Christ's admonition, "Listen to me, all of you, and understand: there is nothing outside a person that by going in can defile, but the things that come out are what defile" (Mark 7:14–15), and in a tradition that has great reverence for the body, it is shocking to hear childbirth described as something that makes a mother's body and spirit "impure," "defiled," or "stained," and worthy of investigation as to why this is the case.

"All Things Are Pure"

To evaluate impurity language, we must take a little journey through theological understandings of impurity throughout Christian history. First, as Christians accepted the Hebrew Scriptures that became known to them as the Old Testament, they began to read it through a new, Christian lens. This required Christians to reckon with Levitical law, the various rules about righteous living listed in the Book of Leviticus that Moses gave to the Israelites. Among the laws presented in Leviticus are instructions for ritual action to take place after childbirth (Lev 12:1–8): for example, an "unclean" woman must wait forty days before returning to the temple if her child is a boy (longer if she has a girl) and bring particular animals for sacrifice, in order to be "clean" again. In the ancient Israelite context, simply put, this sort of "uncleanliness" or "impurity" referred to a state in which the divine equilibrium was out of kilter but could be made right again through ritual action.

But this was not the understanding of purity given by Jesus Christ, who fulfilled the law (Matt 5:17–20) and recast "impurity" into the category of sinful language or actions. Jesus underscored this very point with regard to women when he allowed the woman with the issue of blood—who was certainly suffering from a menstrual disorder—to *touch him*, something well outside the bounds of the ritual purity laws of Leviticus. This was also not the understanding of "impurity" largely held by the early church, as reflected by Saint John Chrysostom: "All things are pure. God made nothing unclean, for nothing is unclean, except in sin only. For that reaches to the soul and defiles it. Other uncleanness is human prejudice."[4]

But, alongside this shift in the understanding of impurity in the early church, there were some Christian thinkers for whom women's bodies were the one exception to the inapplicability of Levitical law. The new Christian understanding of impurity as sinfulness, combined with a trend toward an appreciation of consecrated virginity over family life, meant that women's bodies—particularly their childbearing-related fluids, menstruation and lochia—were directly linked with sin, especially by such figures as Origen and Tertullian.[5] This thinking is demonstrated by an early Christian text that instructs a new mother returning to church to stand with the catechumens (those seeking to join the church, but who were not yet baptized), indicating that her status as a baptized Christian was compromised as a consequence of giving birth.[6]

In response to those who wished to stigmatize women's bodies, other parts of the early church pointedly maintained that women's bodies are not impure. For example, the *Apostolic Constitutions* from fourth-century Syria, an early guidebook of sorts for Christian living, states, "For neither lawful mixture, nor child-bearing, nor the menstrual purgation, nor nocturnal pollution, can defile the nature of a man [*sic*], or separate the Holy Spirit from him [*sic*]. Nothing but impiety and unlawful practice can do that. For the Holy Spirit always abides with those that are possessed of it, so long as they are worthy."[7] There is no disruption of the divine equilibrium, no distance from God, no sin prompted by childbirth or menstruation in this formulation. Interestingly, "nocturnal emissions"—the involuntary nighttime ejaculation of men—is also mentioned in this particular document, demonstrating that not all Christian exceptions to Levitical law were about women; there was occasionally a wider focus on the body and its sexual functions. However, nocturnal emissions get nowhere near the amount of attention in the tradition that was accorded to menstruation and childbirth, and there is certainly not a public rite for this situation (though there are private prayers).

John Chrysostom spoke specifically to childbirth, saying that "those things are not polluted which arise from nature [meaning conception and childbirth]...but those which arise from choice."[8] Here, Chrysostom asserts that sin has nothing to do with biology but everything to do with one's own free will. He clearly understands matters involving women, sexuality, and childbirth as part of what was fulfilled by the coming of Jesus Christ, meaning that they are not subject to purification requirements. Chrysostom is making this argument in the context of rather roughly rejecting what he calls "Judaizers" in the church, those Christians who wish to institute their notions of Levitical law, so there is some polemical intent in the context of this passage. But his thinking holds true outside of this combative context, and the conviction that the law pertaining to women's bodies is just as fulfilled as any other part of the Levitical inheritance is, in most times and places, the accepted thinking of the church. This is especially true in the Christian East, where connections between sex, menstruation, and childbirth and impurity are the minority report.

Even so, the theologically poor understanding of purity that has to do not so much with Levitical law as with sin associated with sex, conception, and women's bodies made its way into the churching prayers.

"Impurity": An Unwelcome Innovation

Significantly, the oldest texts of churching prayers from the Christian East are from the eighth century, and they do not include any impurity language. Indeed, they do not include prayers for the mother—these early rites are exclusively focused on the baby. It seems likely that these prayers developed out of a need to give infants—who came to church with their mothers as nursing babes-in-arms—a proto-Christian sort of status; these little people were not yet baptized (they would be soon), and so they needed some sort of official status in order to be present in church, given that unbaptized adults were not allowed to stay for the full liturgy at this time.

That the early churching prayers on record lack any connection between impurity and childbirth is especially interesting because it suggests that there was not a continuous ritual tradition from Mary's purification (Luke 2:22–38, celebrated on February 2 in both Christian East and West) through the early Christian era, which would be the logical ritual connection. Nor was there a ritual connection, it seems, with the celebration of this feast, which was inaugurated as early as the fourth century. Instead, the church truly did honor the conviction that childbirth is not sinful and that purification after childbirth is not necessary in its postpartum practices; for the first twelve hundred years of the Eastern church, no rite was established to define an end to the postpartum period and no mention was made of impurity and childbirth when new mothers came back to church. This state of affairs apparently changed in the twelfth century, when the prayers that were initially used exclusively to welcome the baby to church were expanded to include references to the mother, including her putative impurity.[9]

In the Christian West, things unfolded differently. The first churching prayers of any kind were focused almost entirely on the mother instead of the baby, and immediately included the connection with impurity—barely predating the introduction of impurity language into the Eastern churching prayers. The Western prayers contained various readings from the Book of Psalms and called for the priest to lead the woman into church by the hand while reciting a prayer that unambiguously asks for her purification from sin in the wake of childbirth. He later sprinkled her with holy water and censed her, actions that symbolize her purification. A typical twelfth-century text includes the prayer that the mother be freed *ab omni sorde peccati et immundicia cordis et corporis* ("from the impurity of the heart and the stain of all sin of the body").[10]

While I cannot do this topic justice here, I will simply note that the thinking on sexuality and bodies by such figures as the abovementioned Origen and Tertullian informed the thinking of Augustine who was enormously influential in the Christian West, and that this connection between childbirth and impurity took an earlier and firmer hold in the West. Even though, on the whole, the thinking on sexuality and bodies was more positive in the East, the putative connection between impurity and childbirth gained some steam in the late Byzantine era, hence the addition of the concept of impurity into the churching prayers.

There are probably several reasons for this. For one, this era is marked by an interest in ritual particularity: everything from the regulation of sacred space to the clergy's preparation for the liturgy received a lot of attention in canon law and church thought. Relatedly, there was also an uptick in interest in a very sin-focused and body-denying form of Christian-interpreted Levitical law that was most certainly not a revival of an ancient understanding of ritual purity, but was, instead, an intentional association between sin and impurity. Notably, this was also the era in which the ordained female diaconate ceased to exist in the East, partly on the premise that menstruation ought to exclude women from the altar. This meant there were no longer women in the clergy, and thus no women were close to any of the decisions made about changing these prayers. Whatever the influence, the introduction of impurity into the Orthodox postpartum prayers constituted an innovation. I wonder if the natural ebb and flow of liturgical change would have washed this language out of the prayers had the printing press not appeared on the scene not too long after this language appeared in the rites, which effectively ensconced impurity in these rites to the present day.

The innovative addition of impurity to the churching prayers sticks out like a sore thumb today. Within the Orthodox Church today, there is an appreciation for family, motherhood, and childbearing, thanks in part to the translation of the homilies of Saint John Chrysostom that are dedicated to familial topics, and which, as seen, include his rejection of any association between impurity and childbearing. Therefore, the language of impurity falls hard on a new mother's ears—and the ears of her husband and the rest of the parish. While past generations might have been more accepting of the perceived authority of the prayer book, today the faithful are educated and recognize the association between childbirth and impurity as in jarring contradiction to everything else they have been told about Christian family life and the holiness of the human body.

It is not just laypeople that are perturbed by these prayers; there is a widespread reluctance among clergy to praying them as they are written. It is not unheard of for Orthodox priests to change the language of churching on the fly—something done with no other liturgical service. Priests sometimes offer, as mine did with my second child, to say the prayers in a language that the mother does not understand so she does not have to hear the words, which is truly indicative of something awry, as Orthodox prayers are always in the vernacular.

Churching in the Hands of Mothers

I have said much about the theologically poor and spiritually damaging connection between impurity and childbirth in the churching prayers. More egregious, however, is the concomitant rejection of the church's understanding of the body contained in these prayers, because when the theology of the body is disregarded, the premise for the theology of the body is also at risk: the understanding that God became human; that he himself took on a human body. The putative impurity present in the churching prayers disparages the goodness of the human body, as sanctified by the incarnation. The problems with the churching prayers are not just "women's problems"; they are problems universal to the church's theology and deserving the attention of the whole church.

Of universal importance as well is certain language used to describe Mary that needs to be reconsidered in light of the Christian understanding of impurity and purity. When we refer to her, as we often do, as "All Pure One," then "pure" can be understood as "without sin," reflecting the Christian use of the concept of purity and the Orthodox understanding that Mary, through her own free will, lived a holy life. When words like "corruption" are applied to Mary's childbirth, however, the meaning is less clear, as in a hymn sung at the beginning and end of many services: "More honorable than the Cherubim and more glorious beyond compare than the Seraphim, without corruption you gave birth to God the Word, true Theotokos we magnify you."[11] "Defilement" is often used in place of "corruption." With either word choice, it might be easy to conclude that normal human childbirth would have been the source of corruption or defilement of Mary, but she dodged that bullet by giving birth to God.

But I do not believe this is the most fruitful understanding of this language in reference to Mary. Sometimes when these words are applied to Mary they are intended to refer to her virginity during her birthgiving, meaning her intact anatomy, and, as noted in the previous chapter, this understanding of her birthgiving experience is not the only one within the Orthodox tradition. Most powerfully, though, Mary's "incorruption" or lack of "defilement" also refers to the sheer wonder of the fact that a human mother was able to bear God in her womb—that something impossible was made possible. In this way, Mary is often likened in Orthodoxy to the burning bush that Moses saw in the desert that was not consumed (corrupted or defiled), also an impossible reality, and it is this meaning that needs to be reclaimed regarding Mary.

Fortunately, the theology, language, and pastoral consequences of the churching prayers are being reconsidered in some parts of the Orthodox Church. Bishops are blessing the publication of churching prayers in which the impurity references are optional.[12] Although churching can be and is used for adopted children, new prayers are being crafted that speak more specifically to the welcoming of a new child and a new mother into the church in the case of adoption, which might not be, after all, directly on the heels of childbirth, which is the situation assumed in the churching prayers. The role the father and the godparents ought to play in these rites is being considered, as well.

These changes are good and very much welcome. As I have noted, there is wisdom in marking when a woman remerges from her birthgiving experience and returns to her normal routine by first coming to church, and churching contains the possibility of functioning as a beautiful liturgical rite of hospitality for new mothers. Furthermore, often it is the case that the prayers in churching are the very first and very last things a woman hears her church say about motherhood; these prayers are a catechesis for motherhood. It is therefore critically important for the churching prayers to do justice to the church's theology of the body, and thus the maternal body.

Given the structure of the Orthodox Church, most of these changes to the churching prayers are being made and approved by men—priests in parishes and metropolitan offices, bishops approving translations and new prayer books, and so forth. Their efforts are laudable and very welcome. Yet, would it not be wonderful and appropriate for theologically trained women, especially those who have given birth and then walked back through the narthex doors to rejoin their community with an infant in their arms, to recraft the churching prayers? This is not to suggest that the church's male clergy have nothing to offer new mothers, but it is to say that it is *fitting* for mothers to pen these prayers, given their history and given the fact that mothers understand what the postpartum time period is like in a way that the male clergy simply cannot, no matter how sympathetic, well-intentioned, or pastorally gifted.

When women, and especially mothers, compose revised prayers for churching, I believe these prayers will authentically reflect the church's longstanding esteem for mothers, childbirth, the human person, and the human body. These prayers will then include all the things that mothers ought to hear from their church when they return to this community for the first time after childbirth—be that everything from welcome, to praise, to celebration of birthgiving and new life, to thanksgiving for having endured pregnancy and childbirth, to preservation of the well-being of the maternal body, to beseeching strength and wisdom for the many days of motherhood to come. In the hands of the church's mother-theologians, the churching prayers will rightly celebrate the maternal body, in all its incarnational glory.

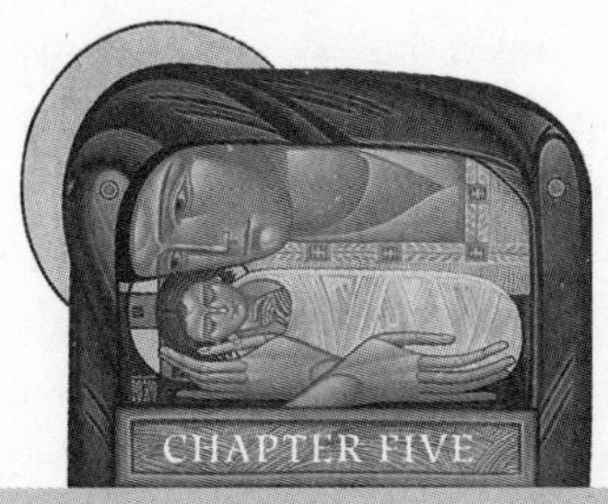

BREASTFEEDING

A mother begins to nurse her newborn soon after childbirth. The baby has an instinctual rooting reflex that means she opens her mouth when she senses the breast nearby. The mother learns to take advantage of that moment, positioning the baby such that her mouth encompasses the entire nipple. It often takes a good deal of trial and error until both parties have the hang of things, and to say this process can be uncomfortable for the mother is an understatement. When all is working smoothly, however, the baby latches right on to the breast, the mother's milk lets down, and they settle in for a session, repeating this process many times a day (and night) during the newborn period. Breastfeeding is part of the postpartum era of motherhood covered in the previous chapter, but the physical act of nourishing another human being by one's own body is so significant to the maternal body that it merits its own consideration.

When it comes to nursing, the maternal body is a wonder. A woman's body is primed for motherhood such that some adoptive mothers of a newborn, who have never given birth before, have nevertheless successfully nursed, just by repeatedly latching their baby on to the breast. For the first few days, colostrum is produced for the baby, a watery milk that is rich in protein and antibodies. The mother's own body changes in response to nursing. Not only do her breasts change shape and size throughout the experience of nursing, but her uterus also responds to nursing-triggered hormones by quickly shrinking back to its normal size. All the while, the effort of producing milk is enormously taxing on the mother's body; the process is so energy intensive that it requires something like 500 calories per day.

For many mothers, breastfeeding is a pleasurable part of the experience of the maternal body, and this was true in my case. My firstborn and I experienced some fumbling and frustration, but we figured it out. By the time my second came around, I knew what I was doing from the beginning and she caught on quickly, too. With the triplets, breastfeeding did not come easily at first; my body was so weary from the pregnancy that my milk was slow to come in. My youngest son, who we all joked was "undercooked" because he was the only one that required an intervention at birth—a half day of supplemental oxygen—took longer to learn to nurse than the others because he simply would not stay awake to eat. But I am nothing if not persistent, and, ultimately, the triplets all nursed.

I happily supplemented with formula, especially when there was someone else available to feed them at night, but they received most of their sustenance from me. When I tell people this, inevitably they look confused and stammer, "But then how could you do anything else?" I didn't. I spent most of my days sitting on the couch nursing one baby after another. There are worse ways to while away a few months.

Like many mothers, I loved the oxytocin rush at the moment of milk letdown—the release of this unique breastfeeding hormone that for me produced a lovely burst of happy calm. Plus, nursing gave me intimate, one-on-one time with each of them, a precious commodity in our family.

Let me acknowledge that nursing does not come easily to every mother. Some mothers do not enjoy it, and there are circumstances and reasons that mean a mother does not breastfeed. None of this undermines the authenticity of her motherhood. Continuing with the orientation of the biological process of motherhood, this chapter pointedly addresses the maternal body of the nursing mother, but this focus in no way diminishes the maternal bodies of mothers who do not breastfeed their babies.

Unlike the other stages of motherhood, there are not reams of interesting and highly visible Orthodox sources on breastfeeding, nor is there any associated rite. There are, however, scriptural and patristic uses of breastfeeding metaphors. For example, Saint Paul positively compares his relationship with the Thessalonians to that of a wet nurse tendering those in her care: "But we were gentle among you, like a nurse tenderly caring for her own children" (1 Thess 2:7).[1] A few hundred years later, John Chrysostom encourages Christians to be as eager for the sustenance of the Eucharist as babies are for the breast: "See ye not the infants with how much eagerness they lay hold of the breast? With what earnest desire they fix their lips upon the nipple? With the like let us also approach this table, and the nipple of the spiritual cup."[2] Chrysostom's frank language here indicates a familiarity with the particulars of breastfeeding, suggesting that women were breastfeeding around him in church, and his positive comparison of the act of receiving communion to that of nursing indicates a favorable opinion of breastfeeding.

There is also an Orthodox icon of breastfeeding that persists across time and space, though it has always been a minority tradition. This is the *Galaktotrophousa* icon, the image of Mary nursing the infant Christ (see Figure 5). *Galaktotrophousa* translates from the Greek as "Milk Feeder" or "Milk Giver." *Galaktotrophousa* shares a root word with *galaxy*, because the Milky Way galaxy—simply *galaxia* in Greek—was understood in Greek mythology as formed by a wayward gush of milk from Hera's breast when she was startled after being tricked into nursing a baby not her own. In a turn of etymological events that delights me, the general term *galaxy* ultimately derived from *galaxia*, and thus our word for a gravitationally related group of stars comes from the life-giving act of breastfeeding.

These cosmic associations with the Milk Giver icon are appropriate, as Mary's nursing of Christ was truly a cosmic act. This is beautifully reflected in a hymn by Saint Ephrem:

> As indeed He sucked Mary's milk,
> He has given suck—life to the universe.
> As again He dwelt in his mother's womb,
> In His womb dwells all creation.[3]

Ephrem celebrates that Christ, who gave life to all of creation, is paradoxically himself given life through Mary's breasts, through her maternal body. This is a cosmic action, and this cosmic action is preserved in the Milk Giver icons, which are some of the most ancient depictions of Mary of any sort and are the focus of this chapter.

An Anomalous Icon

The scriptural narrative of Jesus's childhood contains no mention of Mary nursing him on which to base an icon, but, once again, the *Book of James* provides details where the Gospels are silent: "The infant [Jesus Christ] appeared, and went and took the breast from His mother Mary."[4] It may also well be that this aspect of Jesus and Mary's relationship was an oral tradition, later preserved in visual form. It was certainly typical for Jewish women of the time to nurse their own children, as indicated by the word for infant in Hebrew, *tinok*, meaning "nursling." Thus, it is reasonable to gather that Mary breastfed Jesus.

Jesus tacitly acknowledged this himself in his adulthood. While he was teaching, "a woman in the crowd raised her voice and said to him, 'Blessed is the womb that bore you and the breasts that nursed you!' But he said, 'Blessed rather are those who hear the word of God and obey it!'" (Luke 11:27–28). Some read this as a rebuke of the bonds of blood kinship in favor of the bonds of discipleship. But it can also be understood as a simultaneous celebration of kinship and discipleship; there is no better example of "those who hear the word of God and obey it" than Mary. Perhaps here Jesus is essentially saying, "My mother's holiness is due to her ability to align herself with God just as much as having given birth to me." Indeed, "Blessed is the womb that bore you and the breasts that nursed you!" is sometimes used as an epithet inscribed on Milk Giver icons.

The Milk Giver is an ancient image, dating back to at least the third century from the catacombs of Rome. An image of life-giving in a place of remembering the dead is appropriate for Christians, since we look to the life to come.

Although it has never achieved predominance among images in the Orthodox Church such that it is likely to be found in a typical parish, it persists through the centuries and across geography, in homes, in churches, and in monasteries, including a sixth-century fresco in an Egyptian monastery; an icon from the Judean desert, believed to date from the same time period, that now has its own feast day: the *Hilander Galaktotrophousa*; a twelfth-century mosaic on the façade of the Basilica of Santa Maria in Trastevere in Rome; in many popular icons in seventeenth-century Russia; and today in contemporary versions sold online in the United States. This persistent but never popular presence of the Milk Giver is important to keep in mind in the consideration of the depiction of Mary's maternal body in the icon.

Because there is no scriptural setting for this icon, it includes no narrative details like the icons for the Visitation or the Nativity; the Milk Giver icon, as its name implies, simply shows Mary nursing Jesus. The eighteenth-century Greek example includes a bit of adornment—Mary is being crowned by two archangels and her halo is delicately ornamented in a floral pattern—but it is otherwise typical for a Milk Giver icon. Mary is holding Jesus, who is clearly nursing from her right breast, which is peeking out from behind her robe. His little hand rests on her breast, in a manner that suggests a baby at ease, and Mary herself looks quite peaceful. There are no surprises here in terms of this being a depiction of a mother and child nursing; all of this makes visual and anatomical sense—except for the lactating breast itself.

The position of the breast is anatomically amiss. It is located awkwardly high on her chest, looking as though it originates from Mary's arm or armpit. The size of her breast is typically well out of scale with the rest of her; it is too small, maybe a quarter of the size it ought to be, even allowing for the natural variation in breast size among women, and the shape is oddly conical. The depiction of Mary's breast in the Milk Giver icons is not faithful to the reality of her maternal body, or to any maternal body.

This is awry. As noted in chapter 2, icons show saints in a stylized but embodied form. The stylization of Orthodox icons means that faces are elongated, clothing is draped a certain way, and so on, and is meant to suggest the deification of the saint. However, saint's bodies are shown anatomically correct, and honoring the human form is central to Orthodox iconography and theology. The Milk Giver icon is the only icon of which I know that includes a purposefully misplaced and misrepresented body part.

In contrast, during the early Renaissance, the Christian West had no hesitation about depicting an anatomically correct Mary nursing her son. *Madonna Lactans* or *Virgo Lactans* paintings show the nursing breast in the correct place and the correct size. Sometimes she and Christ are shown taking a break from nursing, with him looking into her eyes, or at the viewer. In these paintings, the breast itself is often exposed, and painted realistically and with great detail—a composition not found in the Milk Giver icons of the Christian East.

But this presentation of an authentic maternal body in the Christian West was not to last—the Council of Trent in the mid-sixteenth century issued guidelines about religious images that changed the way Mary was to be represented in the future: "Moreover, in the invocation of saints, the veneration of relics, and the sacred use of images, every superstition shall be removed, all filthy lucre be abolished; finally, all lasciviousness be avoided; in such wise that figures shall not be painted or adorned with a beauty exciting to lust."[5] Sadly, an image of Mary nursing Christ that includes a visible breast was deemed as possibly inciting "lasciviousness" or "lust," and therefore fell out of use in the Christian West. It seems that neither East nor West was ultimately able to faithfully depict Mary's maternal body.

Looking East again, the style of the Milk Giver remained remarkably consistent over time, with the breast misshapen and out of place. To consider why this might be the case, and the theological implications of this stray breast, first an overview of the theories of the origin and meaning of the Milk Giver icon is in order.

"Who Are You?": Divinized Maternity

As noted, it is reasonable to conclude that Mary nursed Jesus, and on this basis, it makes sense that a Milk Giver icon might appear in Christian imagery. However, breastfeeding practices in the Christian communities that created and venerated Milk Giver icons varied in the first millennium. Some Roman women of means sent their infants to wet nurses who were either household slaves or lower-class women who were nominally compensated, and yet there are writings from the same era—composed by men—extolling the womanly virtues of breastfeeding one's own child. It may have been the case that the wealthy Christians sponsoring and viewing the iconography in their church had not themselves experienced breastfeeding.

Perhaps because of the mixed attitudes toward breastfeeding in the larger culture, or because the Milk Giver icon appeared persistently in different places without ever gaining universal popularity, this icon prompts a good deal of speculation. Some suggest that the early depictions of Mary nursing Christ mimic depictions of the Egyptian goddess Isis nursing Horus, an image that was common throughout the ancient world. In this thinking, iconographers, either consciously or unconsciously, chose a depiction of Mary that was a graceful segue into the Christian sphere for those accustomed to seeing the nursing Isis, and thus immediately ascribed to Mary a certain status.[6] Early Christians did have a proclivity for baptizing pagan images into the fold and reinterpreting them in a Christian spirit, but this does not explain the Milk Giver's enduring popularity well beyond the influence and presence of Isis. This also does not explain Mary's misshapen anatomy in the icon, since the surviving statues of Isis show her breasts proportionally and anatomically appropriate.

Rather than originally forming as an Isis-inspired image, other commentators on the Milk Giver icon believe that it developed as the ultimate witness to Christ's humanity: here is a baby, nursing with his mother. What is more human? This thinking about the Milk Giver icon is a popular contemporary pastoral explanation, and sometimes a caveat is tacked on to explain the odd location of Mary's nursing breast: yes, the icon is a defense of Jesus Christ's humanity, but Mary's breast is portrayed in a distorted way so that the viewer is not scandalized. For example, "The icon is not painted to dwell upon the sensuality of Mary breastfeeding Jesus Christ, merely to proclaim it happened."[7] Out of fear of "dwelling" on Mary's "sensuality," her body is deformed, so this thinking goes.

Others suggest that, given the unlikely setting for some of these Milk Giver images such as male monasteries, the intention of these icons was to bring to mind neither Christ's humanity nor Mary's breastfeeding of Christ at all, but to instead remind viewers of the more metaphorical use of nursing and milk metaphors, such as the ones earlier cited from Apostle Paul and Saint John Chrysostom, calling to mind such ideas as the milk of immortality offered by Christ himself.[8] This explanation relies on early Christian formulas that connect blood (as in uterine blood, in this case) and milk, and it requires a certain leap of faith to connect these formulas with the painted image itself, but, if this were the case, it might explain the anatomical anomaly, as then it could be understood as intended deliberately to evoke a nonphysical interpretation of Mary's nursing of Christ.

Beyond the christological statements and metaphors about the Eucharist, there is another way of viewing the Milk Giver icon: as a more straightforward image of Mary, in her maternal body, nursing her son. Thomas Arentzen arrives at such a conclusion regarding the sixth-century hymnist Romanos the Melodist's descriptions of Mary nursing in Romanos's "Hymns on the Nativity"; Arentzen understands the descriptions of Mary nursing as portraits of Mary's maternity.

For example, Romanos has the magi asking in wonder these questions of Mary when they visit her in the cave:

> Who are you,
> Since you have given birth to someone like this?
> Who is your father? Who bore you,
> Since you have become Mother and Nurse of a
> fatherless son?[9]

Arentzen's reading of this language and other references to Mary in the hymns of Romanos is that it is Mary who is being honored here; the magi are expressing their wonder at Mary's intimate contact with God in the context of her maternal body "since she has become mother and nurse" of Jesus Christ. Addressing the ways in which hymns and images of Mary nursing are often explained as making a doctrinal statement in defense of Christ's humanity, Arentzen observes, "It is true that the physical bonds between Mary and Christ point to his humanity, and that the physical bonds give way to likeness, but we must not reverse the logic of theosis. When God and human beings comingle, it is normally not God who is humanized, but the human who is divinized."[10] I spoke above to the profundity of a mother being able to nourish another human being through her own body. Here, Mary is nourishing God, and this is not just the wonderful, cosmic paradox in which Ephrem delights of human and God each sustaining the other; it is also a situation in which Mary is herself growing in communion with God. The Milk Giver icon can be understood as a depiction of Mary's maternity, which includes her experience of deification in and through her maternal body.

In chapter 3, I referred to the Orthodox Church's diverse ways of expressing Mary's childbirth experience and suggested the importance in maintaining a vision of, without compromising her perpetual virginity, her physically human (not supernatural) birthgiving. At the same time, Mary is the most deified human being. Her experience of deification was through her personal holiness, her consent at the Annunciation, and *through her maternal body*, including through nursing her son. Arentzen notes that Romanos's hymns "stress the divinized maternity of a nursing mother."[11] This is what

Arentzen hears in Romanos's hymns, and this is what I see in the Milk Giver icons—but imperfectly.

Mary's misshapen maternal body fits neither with the iconographic tradition's reverence for the body, nor with the church's understanding that deification begins in the body. Therefore, on display in the Milk Giver icons is another way the church has not integrated the maternal body into its theology of the body. In order for divinized maternity to be fully reflected in icon form, Mary's body must be shown as a real, faithful maternal body, not as a disfigured one—for whatever reason.

The Milk Giver icon maintains an infrequent, but persistent, presence in the Christian East. This indicates that it has enduring appeal, even if the story of its prototype and doctrinal connections are unclear, even if it is anatomically anomalous. Without wanting to presume too much or cast too broad a blanket over this icon's history, this persistence suggests to me that the image of Mary nursing her son speaks to Christians. Perhaps it is the physicality of her relationship with Jesus, her maternal body that holds enduring appeal—skewed as the representation of it may be in the Milk Giver icons.

The popularity of this image is only increasing today, as indicated by the numerous Milk Giver icons for offer in the icon marketplace and the fact that more iconographers are creating this type of icon. Some of these Milk Giver icons are moving in the direction of an anatomically correct Mary; her breast seems to be traveling to a more natural position over time. Iconography is not an art of innovation. There are ancient prototypes of each icon, sometimes with a variant or two, to which iconographers throughout the ages adhere. This is part of the majesty of icons, and it is no small wonder to consider that John Chrysostom himself, for example, saw images of Mary that are nearly identical to the one hanging next to me as I write.

So, I take the continuity of this tradition very seriously when I hope that this trend continues, and that an adjustment to the depiction of Mary in the Milk Giver icons occurs. The church maintains that deification happens through the body, not despite the body, so let the maternal body be shown as it is. I am convinced that a Milk Giver icon with an anatomically correct Mary shown nursing Christ is appropriate, and necessary to honor her incarnation, her maternal body. Offering this example of deification in and through the maternal body will bring some fresh air to the sentiment expressed in 1 Timothy: "Yet she will be saved through childbearing" (2:15).

A Feast for Weaning

Although a mother never stops being a mother, breastfeeding does come to an end. For some mothers this is an orchestrated end, due to a return to work, or a trip, or other factors. For others, the regularity of nursing slowly diminishes as their baby begins to eat more solid food and breastfeeding just tapers off over time. The latter was the case for me with the triplets. The girls lost interest within a day of each other, and my youngest son nursed for just a couple of weeks longer. It was time, it was mutual, but I was more than a little wistful, knowing that he would be the last baby I nursed.

More than that, I also knew that this era of my life was definitively over. I was leaving behind the intensity of early motherhood. I would not again spend a week or two in anticipation, wondering if my husband and I had managed to conceive, nor feel the rocking of another being afloat on the amniotic ocean inside of me, nor give birth and experience all of the changes to my physical being entailed and the reflection prompted, nor be churched as I reemerged into the world once more. These parts of my life were forever past, although my maternal body was forever marked and shaped by them.

This was deeply bittersweet. I would miss all of these things, but I also rejoiced in the increasing independence of the triplets. With each month that passed, the ratio of intense labor to enjoyment on my part shifted farther in the right direction. They were beginning to talk and walk—a stage of motherhood that I find very gratifying, as they issued new communications to me (and each other!) each day. They were flourishing. The more they grew, the more mirthful they became. My older children were delighting in the growth of their triplet siblings and growing up themselves. We were all moving to a new stage of being.

I wondered about the passage in Genesis when Abraham celebrates Isaac's weaning: "The child grew, and was weaned; and Abraham made a great feast on the day that Isaac was weaned" (21:8). How did Sarah feel about Isaac's weaning? Was it a joyful, festive experience of unalloyed gladness for her, or did she, too, feel bittersweet about all the changes it signified, including the changes to her maternal body and the growth of her son?

Weaning signifies more than just the end of the physical mother-child breastfeeding relationship. It is a hallmark of independence of the child and a goodbye of sorts, and it is a fact that motherhood is full of goodbyes. As I write this, my family is preparing for what in our culture today is considered the ultimate metaphorical act of weaning: I will drop my oldest son off at college. I will soon get in a car with him, drive eight hundred miles, unload his books, and his sheets, and his skis, and then turn around and drive home. Will I want to "make a great feast" to mark the occasion? I am truly excited for him and his future, but, at the same time, I can hardly imagine not seeing him every day. I do not know if I will want to feast—or fast. I do know I will experience it not abstractly, not just in my mind, but in my body—in my maternal body.

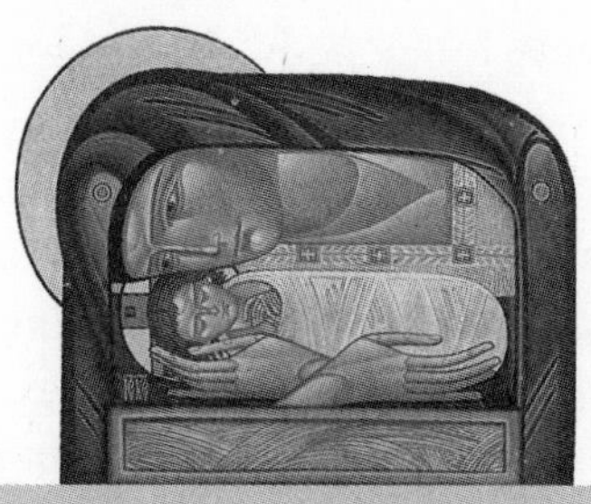

EPILOGUE

A young Orthodox mother recently asked me why so few mothers are listed as saints in the Orthodox Church. The biographies of most mother saints might give her pause, too: many of them became nuns as soon as their children were grown or are like Saint Sophia, who is celebrated for watching her children be martyred before herself experiencing the same fate. It is not easy to find a mother saint who simply lived her life as a mother, without the renunciation of family life for monasticism or the premature end of maternal life in martyrdom, but I assured this young mother, the church does not make saints, it just recognizes them. Given that saints are understood as people who radiantly and profoundly embody the image of God and see it in others, I have no doubt that there are numerous mother saints whose names are absent from the canons.

This disparity in the representation of mothers in the lists of saints is a poignant example of the ways in which the church either does not acknowledge mothers, or, worse, denigrates mothers and their bodies. But this need not continue; all the necessary ingredients for remedy are at hand and internal to the tradition. The groundwork for greater theological attention to motherhood in the church is already laid, such as the rich imagery of motherhood seen in the Anna and Joachim and Visitation icons or heard in the hymns of Ephrem or Romanos. The church has a robust theology of the body; it is just a matter of the maternal body being integrated into that theology.

For greater theological attention to be given to motherhood, I believe two things are necessary. First, the church must welcome the wisdom and work of mothers, and women more generally, in new ways. The Orthodox Church is at an interesting moment in its history when it comes to women. There is now, for the first time ever, a reasonable quantity of Orthodox women trained in a range of church fields—iconography, canon law, church music, theology, and so forth. But the full offering of their gifts to the church will happen not only because of their training; it will require logistical changes in the institutional church. For example, women theologians and historians can research and propose possible revisions to the churching prayers, but they do not have the authority or the means to enact them; church hierarchs must include women scholars in these efforts. Women iconographers can create and sell their own freestanding work, but they must be blessed and hired by church authorities to paint frescoes in church interiors. Women can train as theologians, but there is no certainty that their work will find a home in the church (rather than just the academy), unless the church makes a home for it by hiring them as seminary professors or appointing them as theological advisors. While there are examples of church-blessed female iconographers and church-appointed female theologians, they are rare indeed, and their numbers are small in comparison to the trained and gifted women who are waiting in the wings.

The second requirement I see for greater attention to motherhood is that mothers themselves must do this work—mothers who create icons and find ways to be faithful to both the tradition and to the maternal body; mothers who become theologians and address the theological lacunae of motherhood; and mothers who carve a space for themselves, and an appreciation for motherhood, in the institutional church. The church will see and appreciate its mothers anew when they enter into these aspects of church life, and perhaps more mother saints will then be noticed and named as such.

The work on motherhood within the church *needs to be done by mothers*. This is not to say that it must be exclusively done by mothers. There will be male scholars who have much to offer the history of the churching prayers, bishops who are pastorally talented at ministering to women who have miscarried, women who are not mothers who create inspiring Nativity icons, and so forth. However, the church has not, to date, paused to listen to its mothers' voices, and now is the time to do so. The church has failed to live up to its own theological ideals when it comes to the lives of mothers, and now is the time to remedy this, and those who live those lives ought to be deeply involved. Mothers must do the work of bringing motherhood into the theological conversation of the church because no one else will do it for them. Finally, this work must be done by mothers because they alone experience motherhood, and—most germane to this book—they alone know the maternal body, which is unique among human experiences and worthy of reflection.

Let me be clear about what I am *not* suggesting here when I refer to the uniqueness of the maternal body. Those who are not mothers—both male and female—are not disembodied talking heads. But the changeability of the maternal body has no other parallel in human life; no one else endures such dramatic physical transformations under normal circumstances. There is no triumphalism here; this is neither an elevation of the subset of mothers over all other women, nor the conflation of motherhood with womanhood. Rather, noting the maternal body's uniqueness and importance is one avenue of appreciation for this understudied aspect of human experience. The claim that the maternal body is unique is also not a reductive claim; this is no relegation of mothers (or women) to a cliché of mother-earthy metaphors. It is simply the case that motherhood—in whatever biological or adoptive shape it comes—inevitably entails an elemental embodiment, giving mothers a singular incarnational reality.

The unique incarnational reality of mothers recalls more general discussions in theological circles today around the ultimate meaning of man and woman. One question is whether sex differentiation is part of our created state such that it defines our very person, our very soul. This is not an area where we can consult the wisdom of the early church thinkers for answers—these are questions of our time, not theirs. Some of the essential definitions of male and female offered seem to split humanity into two species and elevate male-female sex distinction over personhood. But it seems to me that the unique human person, created in the image and likeness of God, is the first principle from which we must operate when considering these things.

However, I do believe that our lived experience of male and female *has meaning*. Our personal incarnational reality carries weight, so to speak, and this conviction is one of the truest, most enduring observations of Christianity. This is true for us as male and female, it is true for us in our personal and cultural experience of gender over time, it is true for us as individual persons in our own unique bodies, and this is true for mothers in their maternal bodies. The incarnational reality of the maternal body is meaningful, and yet mothers' bodies are not integrated into the theological body of the church.

Until recently, much of the theological work of the church was done by people with a circumscribed incarnational reality: celibate men, who know neither the intimacies of sexual relations within marriage, nor the challenges of parenthood, much less the experience of the maternal body. For a tradition that honors the body and understands it to be the location of one's path to deification, this is a very narrow perspective on the body. For a church that is predicated on a birth, whose God enters this world through his mother's body, this is ironically incongruous.

Theological work on motherhood is obviously important and necessary for mothers, but I believe it is also necessary for the church. For the church as a body to be whole, its maternal bodies must be seen, considered, honored, and included. Just as the Apostle Paul tells us that if one member suffers, the whole body suffers, it is also true that if one member is appreciated, then the whole body will benefit: "If one member is honored, all rejoice together with it" (1 Cor 12:26). The changing nature of the maternal body, its ability to metamorphose over time, through conception, pregnancy, birth, postpartum, and breastfeeding—perhaps repeating this process many times in one lifetime, but with the experience never exactly the same—serves as a valuable and evocative reminder of our incarnate, embodied human nature to all of us: no matter when or how we became mothers, or if we are mothers at all. May the church honor the unique incarnate reality of the maternal body, learn from it, and thus rejoice!

Furthermore, the maternal body signifies other things on which I have barely touched—for example, its fluid mutability works against the lie of the linearity of time. In its cycles of life-giving and life-sustaining, the maternal body points to the ways that time folds in upon itself, much as in the cycles of the liturgical year. Yes, chronological time does keep marching on, but there is a deeper sense of time that is lived out in the maternal body. Some say that Christian life is understood as a series of deaths and resurrections. It can also be understood as a series of births and returns, and the maternal body reveals this sense of ever-renewal.

This is a speculative, suggestive, nascent, and imperfect theology of the body. In it, I celebrate aspects of my beloved Orthodox Church, and question others. I try to avoid dogmatism, even when my church strays from its own incarnational body. I wonder how the church will change as more women and mothers enter the theological stream. I imaginatively describe and explore the maternal body and hold it up as offering a new way of considering the church's theology of the body. My hope is that *Maternal Body* will be just one of many theological works on motherhood within the church.

My experience of motherhood is the most life-giving and renewing experience of my life. I brought five new humans into the world, and that was no small part of it, but there is also a way in which *I* was reborn with the births of each of my children. Reborn in the sense that my body was so altered by pregnancy and childbirth that I was embodied anew, and reborn in the sense that the entire experience of my maternal body is one of deeply inhabiting my own incarnational reality, living in the body that was fashioned by my Creator, that is shaped by my motherhood, and that is called to eternity.

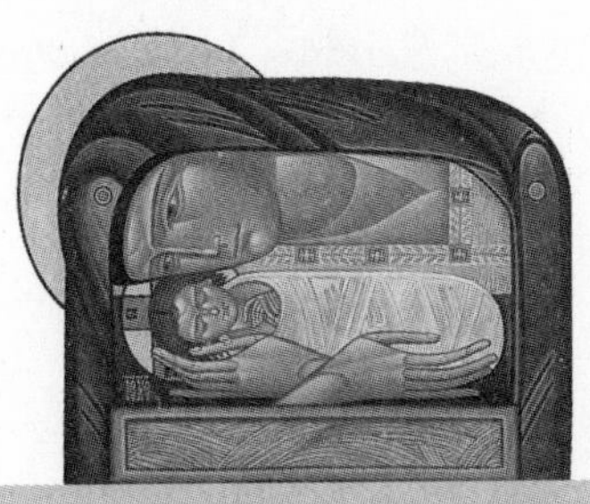

NOTES

Preface

1. “Divine Liturgy of Saint John Chrysostom,” Greek Orthodox Archdiocese of America, https://www.goarch.org/chapel/texts/-/asset_publisher/ulcNzWPdScz6/content/the-divine-liturgy-of-saint-john-chrysostom?_101_INSTANCE_ulcNzWPdScz6_languageId=en_US.

2. Jerome, “Letter 108,” rev. and ed. for New Advent by Kevin Knight, 2009, accessed September 24, 2018, http://www.newadvent.org/fathers/3001108.htm.

3. Maureen Fiedler, “Pope Francis on Women in His Interview with *America* Magazine,” *National Catholic Reporter*, September 19, 2013, http://ncronline.org/blogs/francis-chronicles/pope-francis-women-his-interview-america-magazine.

4. Basil of Caesarea, “On the Origin of Humanity, Discourse, 1,” in *On the Human Condition*, trans. Nonna Verna Harrison (Crestwood, NY: St. Vladimir’s Seminary Press, 2005), 45.

5. Athanasius, *On the Incarnation* 8, rev. and ed. for New Advent by Kevin Knight, accessed September 25, 2018, http://www.newadvent.org/fathers/2802.htm.

6. Irenaeus, *Against Heresies,* Book V, Preface, rev. and ed. for New Advent by Kevin Knight, accessed September 25, 2018, http://www.newadvent.org/fathers/0103500.htm.

Chapter One

1. John Chrysostom, "Homily 12 on Colossians 4:18," in *On Marriage and Family Life*, trans. Catherine P. Roth and David Anderson (Crestwood, NY: St. Vladimir's Seminary Press, 1986), 76.

2. "Kontakion for Conception of the Honorable and Glorious Prophet, Forerunner, and Baptist John," Orthodox Church in America, accessed September 25, 2016, https://oca.org/saints/troparia/2018/09/23/102703-conception-of-the-honorable-glorious-prophet-forerunner-and-bapt.

3. "Holy Matrimony," Orthodox Church in America, 2013, accessed September 25, 2018, https://oca.org/PDF/Music/Marriage/marriage-service.pdf.

4. *The Protoevangelium of James*, 1, rev. and ed. for New Advent by Kevin Knight, 2009, accessed September 26, 2018, http://www.newadvent.org/fathers/0847.htm.

5. *The Protoevangelium of James*, 2.

6. *The Protoevangelium of James*, 3.

7. *The Protoevangelium of James*, 4.

8. *The Protoevangelium of James*, 4.

9. *The Protoevangelium of James*, 4.

10. "The Conception by Righteous Ann of the Most Holy Mother of God, Kontakion," Orthodox Church in America, accessed September 26, 2015, https://oca.org/saints/troparia/2018/12/09/103506-the-conception-by-righteous-anna-of-the-most-holy-mother-of-god.

11. Vigen Guroian, "An Ethic of Marriage and Family," in *Incarnate Love: Essays in Orthodox Ethics* (Notre Dame, IN: University of Notre Dame Press, 1987), 88.

12. John Chrysostom, "Homily 2 on Hannah," in *Old Testament Homilies*, trans. Robert C. Hill (Brookline, MA: Holy Cross Orthodox Press, 2003), 83.

13. Chrysostom, "Homily 3 on Hannah," in *Old Testament Homilies*, 97.

14. Chrysostom, "Homily 3 on Hannah," in *Old Testament Homilies*, 99.

15. Sigrid Undset, *Kristin Lavransdatter II: The Wife*, trans. Tiina Nunnally (New York: Penguin Classics, 1999), 107.

16. "Prayer for a Woman When She Has Miscarried/Aborted an Infant," in *The Great Book of Needs*, vol. 1 (South Canaan, PA: St. Tikhon's Seminary Press, 2000), 17.

Chapter Two

1. Ephrem the Syrian, "Nativity 4," in *Ephrem the Syrian: Hymns*, trans. Kathleen E. McVey (New York: Paulist Press, 1989), 101.

2. *The Akathist Hymn*, trans. N. Michael Vaporis and Evie Zachariades-Holmberg, Greek Orthodox Archdiocese of America, accessed September 26, 2018, https://www.goarch.org/-/the-akathist-hymn-and-small-compline.

3. See *Apostolic Constitutions* 8.2 X, rev. and ed. Kevin Knight for New Advent, accessed September 26, 2018, http://www.newadvent.org/fathers/07158.htm.

4. This icon can be found in the Greek Orthodox Archdiocese of America's women's Monastery of the Holy Theotokos the Life Giving Spring in Squaw Valley, California, accessed September 26, 2018, http://www.stnicholasranch.org/monastery/.

Chapter Three

1. Alexander Schmemann, "Introduction," in *The Services of Christmas: The Nativity of Our Lord, God, and Savior, Jesus Christ* (Latham, NY: Orthodox Church in America, 1981 and 1983), see http://dce.oca.org/assets/files/resources/117.pdf. For more information about the origins of this feast, see Paul F. Bradshaw and Maxwell E. Johnson, *The Origins of Feasts, Fasts and Seasons in Early Christianity* (Collegeville, MN: Liturgical Press, 2011), 210.

2. Mary B. Cunningham, *Gateway of Life: Orthodox Thinking on the Mother of God* (Yonkers, NY: St. Vladimir's Seminary Press, 2015), 93.

3. "Compline, Forefeast of the Nativity of Christ," in *The Festal Menaion*, trans. Mother Mary and Kallistos Ware (South Canaan, PA: St. Tikhon's Seminary Press, 1990), 206.

4. Ephrem the Syrian, "Nativity 21.21," in *Ephrem the Syrian*, 178.

5. Cunningham, *Gateway of Life*, 105.

6. See *The Protoevangelium of James*, 19.

7. Leonid Ouspensky, "The Nativity of Christ," in Leonid Ouspensky and Vladimir Lossky, *The Meaning of Icons* (Crestwood, NY: St. Vladimir's Seminary Press, 1999), 159.

8. Ouspensky, *The Meaning of Icons*, 159.

9. Kallistos Ware, "Foreword," in Ignatius Brianchaninov, *On the Prayer of Jesus: The Classic Guide to the Practice of Unceasing Prayer Found in the Way of the Pilgrim*, trans. Fr. Lazarus (Boston: New Seeds, 2006), xxix.

10. Jaroslav Pelikan, *Mary Through the Centuries* (New Haven, CT: Yale, 1996), 121.

11. Elisabeth Behr-Sigel, *The Ministry of Women in the Church*, trans. Fr. Steven Bingham (Redondo Beach, CA: Oakwood Publications, 1991), 208.

Chapter Four

1. "Prayers for a Woman on the Fortieth Day of Childbirth," *The Great Book of Needs*, vol. 1 (South Canaan, PA: St. Tikhon's Seminary Press, 2000), 11. I use the English translation of *The Great Book of Needs* that I most frequently encounter in U.S. parishes.

2. "Prayers for a Woman on the Fortieth Day of Childbirth," *The Great Book of Needs*, 10–11.

3. "Prayers for a Woman on the Fortieth Day of Childbirth," *The Great Book of Needs*, 12.

4. John Chrysostom, "Homily 3 on Titus," rev. and ed. for New Advent by Kevin Knight, 2009, accessed September 27, 2018, http://www.newadvent.org/fathers/23083.htm.

5. See Vassa Larin, "What Is 'Ritual Im/purity' and Why?" *St. Vladimir's Theological Quarterly* 52, nos. 3–4 (2008): 275–92.

6. See *The Canons of Hippolytus*, trans. Carol Bebawi, ed. Paul Bradshaw, Alcuin/Grow Liturgical Study 2, Grove Liturgical Study 50 (Bramcote, UK: Grove Books, 1987), 20.

7. *Apostolic Constitutions* 6.28 XXVIII, rev. and ed. for New Advent by Kevin Knight, 2009, accessed October 1, 2018, http://www.newadvent.org/fathers/07156.htm. See also The *Didaskalia Apostolorum*, a third-century Syriac treatise.

8. John Chrysostom, "Homily XXXIII on Hebrews," rev. and ed. for New Advent by Kevin Knight, 2009, accessed October 1, 2018, http://www.newadvent.org/fathers/240233.htm.

9. In the fourteenth-century, current prayers used by the priest on the day after childbirth were added to the service books in addition to churching. "The Prayers on the First Day after a Woman Has Given Birth to a Child" contains the putative link between childbirth and impurity in its earliest textual examples.

10. *Codex Monacensis* 22039 quoted from Susan Roll, "The Churching of Women after Childbirth; An Old Rite Raising New Issues," *Questions Liturgiques* 76 (1995): 216.

11. "Hymn to the Theotokos," Orthodox Church in America, accessed October 1, 2018, https://oca.org/orthodoxy/prayers/hymn-to-the-theotokos.

12. See "Service of Churching of a Woman and Child at Forty Days after Giving Birth," in *Services of Initiation into the Holy Orthodox-Catholic and Apostolic Church*, trans. and ed. Fr. Michel Najim and Fr. Patrick O'Grady (LaVerne, CA: The Antiochian Orthodox Institute, 2017), 17–26.

Chapter Five

1. For a wonderful look at the maternal metaphors in Saint Paul's letters, see Beverly Roberts Gaventa, *Our Mother Saint Paul* (Louisville, KY: Westminster John Knox Press, 2007).

2. John Chrysostom, "Homily 82 on Matthew," rev and ed. for New Advent by Kevin Knight, accessed October 1, 2018, http://www.newadvent.org/fathers/200182.htm.

3. Ephrem the Syrian, "Nativity 4," in *Ephrem the Syrian: Hymns on the Nativity*, trans. Kathleen E. McVey (Mahwah, NJ: Paulist Press, 1989), 101.

4. *Protoevangelium of James*, 19.

5. *The Council of Trent, Twenty-Fifth Session*, ed. and trans. J. Waterworth (London: Dolman, 1848), 235–56, https://history.hanover.edu/texts/trent/ct25.html.

6. See Thomas F. Mathews and Norman Miller, "Isis and Mary in Early Icons," in *Images of the Mother of God: Perceptions of the Theotokos in Byzantium*, ed. Maria Vassilaki (Farnham, UK: Ashgate, 2005), 3–12.

7. "Milk Giver Icon: Not Scandalized by the Incarnation," A Reader's Guide to Orthodox Icons, posted July 3, 2011, accessed October 1, 2018, https://iconreader.wordpress.com/2011/07/03/milk-giver-icon-not-scandalized-by-the-incarnation/.

8. See Elizabeth S. Bolman, "The Enigmatic Coptic Galaktotrophousa and the Cult of the Virgin Mary in Egypt," in *Images of the Mother of God: Perceptions of the Theotokos in Byzantium*, ed. Maria Vassilaki (Farnham, UK: Ashgate, 2005), 13–22.

9. Romanos the Melodist, I 4.5–8, 116, in Thomas Arentzen, *The Virgin in Song: Mary and the Poetry of Romanos the Melodist* (Philadelphia: University of Pennsylvania Press, 2017), 116.

10. Arentzen, *The Virgin in Song*, 110.

11. Arentzen, *The Virgin in Song*, 114.

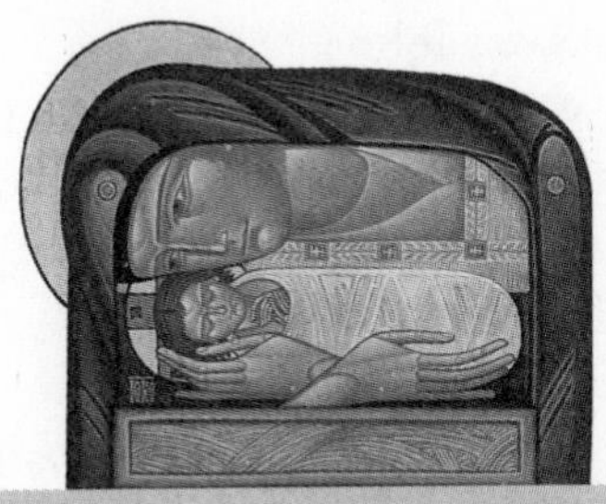

SELECTED BIBLIOGRAPHY

For the convenience of my readers, I chose sources that are available online whenever it was possible and appropriate.

Liturgical Texts

The Akathist Hymn. Translated by N. Michael Vaporis and Evie Zachariades-Holmberg. Greek Orthodox Archdiocese of America. https://www.goarch.org/-/the-akathist-hymn-and-small-compline.

"Compline, Forefeast of the Nativity of Christ." In *The Festal Menaion*, translated by Mother Mary and Kallistos Ware, 204–9. South Canaan, PA: St. Tikhon's Seminary Press, 1990.

"The Conception by Righteous Ann of the Most Holy Mother of God, Kontakion." Orthodox Church in America. https://oca.org/saints/troparia/2018/12/09/103506-the-conception-by-righteous-anna-of-the-most-holy-mother-of-god.

"Divine Liturgy of Saint John Chrysostom." Greek Orthodox Archdiocese of America. https://www.goarch.org/chapel/texts/-/asset_publisher/ulcNzWPdScz6/content/the-divine-liturgy-of-saint-john-chrysostom?_101_INSTANCE_ulcNzWPdScz6_languageId=en_US.

"Holy Matrimony." Orthodox Church in America, 2013. https://oca.org/PDF/Music/Marriage/marriage-service.pdf.

"Hymn to the Theotokos." Orthodox Church in America. https://oca.org/orthodoxy/prayers/hymn-to-the-theotokos.

"Kontakion for Conception of the Honorable and Glorious Prophet, Forerunner, and Baptist John." Orthodox Church in America. https://oca.org/saints/troparia/2018/09/23/102703-conception-of-the-honorable-glorious-prophet-forerunner-and-bapt.

"Prayer for a Woman when She Has Miscarried/Aborted an Infant." In *The Great Book of Needs*, vol. 1, 16–18. South Canaan, PA: St. Tikhon's Seminary Press, 2000.

"Prayers for a Woman on the Fortieth Day of Childbirth." In *The Great Book of Needs*, vol. 1, 10–15. South Canaan, PA: St. Tikhon's Seminary Press, 2000.

"Service of Churching of a Woman and Child at Forty Days after Giving Birth." In *Services of Initiation into the Holy Orthodox-Catholic and Apostolic Church*, translated and edited by Fr. Michel Najim and Fr. Patrick O'Grady, 17–26. LaVerne, CA: The Antiochian Orthodox Institute, 2017.

General Works

Apostolic Constitutions. Revised and Edited for New Advent by Kevin Knight, 2009. http://www.newadvent.org/fathers/07156.htm.

Selected Bibliography

Arentzen, Thomas. *The Virgin in Song: Mary and the Poetry of Romanos the Melodist*. Philadelphia: University Pennsylvania Press, 2017.

Athanasius. *On the Incarnation*. Revised and edited for New Advent by Kevin Knight. http://www.newadvent.org/fathers/2802.htm.

Basil of Caesarea. *On the Human Condition*. Translated by Nonna Verna Harrison. Crestwood, NY: St. Vladimir's Seminary Press, 2005.

Behr-Sigel, Elisabeth. *The Ministry of Women in the Church*. Translated by Fr. Steven Bingham. Redondo Beach, CA: Oakwood Publications, 1991.

Bolman, Elizabeth S. "The Enigmatic Coptic Galaktotrophousa and the Cult of the Virgin Mary in Egypt." In *Images of the Mother of God: Perceptions of the Theotokos in Byzantium*, edited by Maria Vassilaki, 13–22. Farnham, UK: Ashgate, 2005.

Bradshaw, Paul F., and Maxwell E. Johnson. *The Origins of Feasts, Fasts and Seasons in Early Christianity*. Collegeville, MN: Liturgical Press, 2011.

"The Canons of Hippolytus." In *Models of Liturgical Theology*. Grove Liturgical Study 50, translated by Carol Bebawi and edited by Paul F. Bradshaw. Bramcote, Nottingham: Grove Books, 1987.

Chrysostom, John. "Homily 2 on Hannah." In *Old Testament Homilies*, translated by Robert C. Hill. Brookline, MA: Holy Cross Orthodox Press, 2003.

———. "Homily 3 on Titus." Revised and edited for New Advent by Kevin Knight, 2009. http://www.newadvent.org/fathers/23083.htm.

———. "Homily 12 on Colossians 4:18." In *On Marriage and Family Life*, translated by Catherine P. Roth and

David Anderson. Crestwood, NY: St. Vladimir's Seminary Press, 1986.

———. "Homily 82 on Matthew." Revised and edited for New Advent by Kevin Knight. http://www.newadvent.org/fathers/200182.htm.

———. "Homily XXXIII on Hebrews." Revised and edited for New Advent by Kevin Knight, 2009, http://www.newadvent.org/fathers/240233.htm.

Chryssavgis, John. *Love, Sexuality, and the Sacrament of Marriage*. Brookline, MA: Holy Cross Orthodox Press, 1998.

Cunningham, Mary B. *Gateway of Life: Orthodox Thinking on the Mother of God*. Yonkers, NY: St. Vladimir's Seminary Press, 2015.

———. *Wider than Heaven: Eighth-Century Homilies on the Mother of God*. Crestwood, NY: St. Vladimir's Seminary Press, 2008.

Ephrem the Syrian, "Hymns on the Nativity." In *Ephrem the Syrian: Hymns*, translated by Kathleen E. McVey. New York: Paulist Press, 1989.

Evdokimov, Paul. *The Sacrament of Love*. Crestwood, NY: St. Vladimir's Seminary Press, 1985.

———. *Women and the Salvation of the World*. Translated by Anthony P. Gythiel. Crestwood, NY: St. Vladimir's Seminary Press, 1994.

Ford, David C. *Women and Men in the Early Church: The Full Views of St. John Chrysostom*. South Canaan, PA: St. Tikhon's Seminary Press, 1996.

Forest, Jim. *Praying with Icons*. Maryknoll, NY: Orbis Books, 2014.

Gaventa, Beverly Roberts. *Our Mother Saint Paul*. Louisville, KY: Westminster John Knox Press, 2007.

Guroian, Vigen. *Incarnate Love: Essays in Orthodox Ethics*. Notre Dame, IN: University of Notre Dame Press, 1987.

Irenaeus. *Against the Heresies* V. Revised and edited for New Advent by Kevin Knight. http://www.newadvent.org/fathers/0103105.htm.

Jerome, "Letter 108." Revised and edited for New Advent by Kevin Knight, 2009. http://www.newadvent.org/fathers/3001108.htm.

Karras, Valerie. "Patristic Views on the Ontology of Gender." In *Personhood: Orthodox Christianity and the Connection between Body, Mind and Soul*, edited by John T. Chirban. Westport, CT: Bergin and Garvey, 1996.

Larin, Vassa. "What Is 'Ritual Im/purity' and Why?" In *St. Vladimir's Theological Quarterly* 52, nos. 3–4 (2008): 275–92.

Mathews, Thomas F., and Norman Miller. "Isis and Mary in Early Icons." In *Images of the Mother of God: Perceptions of the Theotokos in Byzantium*, edited by Maria Vassilaki, 3–12. Farnham, Great Britain: Ashgate, 2005.

Ouspensky, Leonid, and Vladimir Lossky. *The Meaning of Icons*. Crestwood, NY: St. Vladimir's Seminary Press, 1999.

Pelikan, Jaroslav. *Mary through the Centuries*. New Haven, CT: Yale, 1996.

The Protoevangelium of James. Revised and edited for New Advent by Kevin Knight, 2009. http://www.newadvent.org/fathers/0847.htm.

Roll, Susan. "The Churching of Women after Childbirth; an Old Rite Raising New Issues." In *Questions Liturgiques* 76 (1995): 206–29.

Rubio, Julie Hanlon. *A Christian Theology of Marriage and Family*. Mahwah, NJ: Paulist Press, 2003.

Schmemann, Alexander. "Introduction." In *The Services of Christmas: The Nativity of Our Lord, God, and Savior, Jesus Christ*. Latham, NY: Orthodox Church in America, 1981 and 1983. http://dce.oca.org/assets/files/resources/117.pdf.

Skobtsova, Maria. *Mother Maria Skobtsova: Essential Writings*. Translated by Richard Pevear and Larissa Volokhonsky. Maryknoll, NY: Orbis Books, 2003.

Undset, Sigrid. *Kristin Lavransdatter*. Translated by Tina Nunnally. New York: Penguin Classics, 1999.

Ware, Kallistos. "Foreword." In Ignatius Brianchaninov. *On the Prayer of Jesus: The Classic Guide to the Practice of Unceasing Prayer Found in the Way of the Pilgrim*, translated by Fr. Lazarus, vii–xxxiii. Boston: New Seeds, 2006.

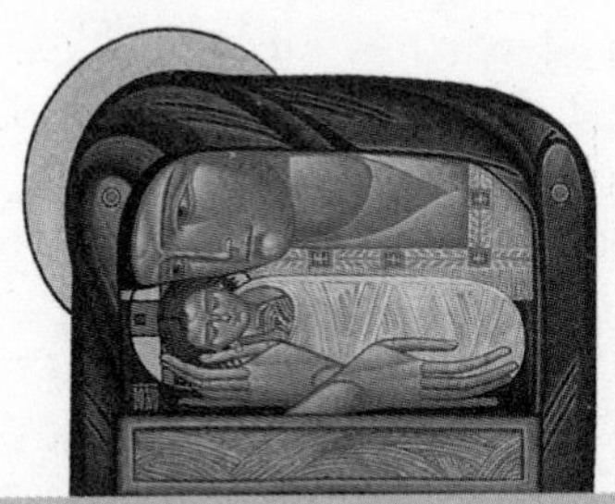

INDEX

Advance Praise for *Maternal Body*

"[This is] a provocative critique and a sensitive reevaluation of the maternal body as it has been depicted in Christian theology, iconography, and liturgical prayer throughout the ages. With passionate conviction, Frost points the way toward a more central role for theologically trained women, female iconographers, and all mothers in the twenty-first-century church. A welcome achievement!"

—Veronica Mary Rolf,
author of *Julian's Gospel: Illuminating the Life and Revelations of Julian of Norwich*

"In bringing a maternal perspective to bear, Frost offers a gentle but incisive critique of aspects of Christian tradition and practice that fall short of the validation of the body created in God's image. At the end she exhorts mothers in the church to speak to and of the faith from their own experience: may many hear her call! And may Frost continue to lead the way."

—Sarah Hinlicky Wilson, author of *Woman, Women, and the Priesthood in the Trinitarian Theology of Elisabeth Behr-Sigel*

"Carrie Frederick Frost draws into her theology of motherhood liturgical hymnody, iconographic imagery, and the deep spirituality of the Orthodox Church, all of this deployed in a compellingly personal exploration of a subject sadly neglected by most feminist theology."

—Vigen Guroian,
author of *The Orthodox Reality: Culture, Theology, and Ethics in the Modern World*